Regent's Study Guides
General Editor: Paul S. Fiddes

Reflections on the Water

*Understanding God and the World
through the Baptism of Believers*

Regent's Study Guides

Reflections on the Water

*Understanding God and the World
through the Baptism of Believers*

Edited by
Paul S. Fiddes

With a response by
Christopher Rowland

Regent's Park College, Oxford

with

Smyth & Helwys Publishing, Inc.®
Macon, Georgia

ISBN (UK) 0-9518104-3-x
ISBN (US) 1-57312-052-9

Reflections on the Water
Understanding God and the World
through the Baptism of Believers

edited by
Paul S. Fiddes

Copyright © 1996

Paul S. Fiddes, Christopher Ellis, Roger Hayden, Brian Haymes,
Richard Kidd, Christopher Rowland, Hazel Sherman
and Regent's Park College, Oxford

Published by Regent's Park College, Oxford OX1 2LB, UK
in association with Smyth & Helwys Publishing, Inc.®
6316 Peake Road, Macon GA 31210-3960, USA

Library of Congress Cataloging-in-Publication Data

Reflections on the water:
    understanding God and the world through the baptism of believers/
    edited by Paul S. Fiddes. (Regent's study guides; 4)
    viii + 144 pp.   6" x 9" (15 x 23 cm.)
    Includes bibliographical references and index.
    ISBN 1-57312-052-9 (alk. paper)
    1. Baptism—Baptists. 2. Baptism—Free churches.
    3. Baptists—Doctrines. 4. Free churches—Doctrines.
    5. Baptism and church membership. 6. Baptism and Christian union.
    I. Fiddes, Paul S. II. Series.
    BV811.2.R44   1996
    234'.161—dc20   96-14324
                                                          CIP

Contents

Notes on Contributors

Christopher Ellis is Minister of Cemetery Road Baptist Church, Shefield, and is chairperson of the Doctrine and Worship Committee of the Baptist Union of Great Britain. Actively engaged in ecumenical relations for many years, he is author of *Together on the Way. A Theology of Ecumenism* (1990).

Paul S. Fiddes is Principal of Regent's Park College at the University of Oxford, and is also a University Research Lecturer. Until recently he was Convenor of the Division for Theology and Education of the European Baptist Federation. Among his publications are *The Creative Suffering of God* (1987), *Past Event and Present Salvation* (1989), and *Freedom and Limit: a Dialogue between Literature and Christian Doctrine* (1991).

Roger Hayden is Superintendent of the Western Area in the Baptist Union of Great Britain. As Vice-President of the Baptist Historical Society, he is the author or editor of several books on Baptist history, including *The Records of the Church of Christ in Bristol, 1640–1687* (1974) and *English Baptist History and Heritage* (1990).

Brian Haymes is Principal of Bristol Baptist College, and is a former President of the Baptist Union of Great Britain. In addition to publications in the areas of Baptist identity and biblical study, he is the author of *The Concept of the Knowledge of God* (1988).

Richard Kidd is Principal of Northern Baptist College, Manchester. Among his many activities in wider spheres of theological education, he is Secretary of the Baptist Colleges Joint Consultative Committee and Editor of the *British Journal of Theological Education*.

Christopher Rowland is Dean Ireland's Professor of Exegesis of Holy Scripture at the University of Oxford, and is a priest in the Church of England. Among his many published works in the area of New Testament study are: *The Open Heaven. A Study of Apocalyptic in Judaism and Early Christianity* (1982), *Christian Origins* (1985), and a commentary on *Revelation* (1993).

Hazel Sherman is the Minister of Kensington Baptist Church, Brecon, having formerly been Tutor in Christian Doctrine at Bristol Baptist College and a Tutor in Theology at Birmingham University.

Acknowledgements

Extracts from the poem by Adrian Mitchell, 'Four for Children', copyright 1964 Adrian Mitchell, and printed in *Poems* (1964), are used by kind permission of the author and Jonathan Cape Ltd., London. Now titled 'Stufferation', the poem is reprinted in *Adrian Mitchell's Greatest Hits—The Top Forty*, published by Bloodaxe Books.

The English translation of an extract from Justin Martyr, Apology for the Christians I, copyright 1957 J. Stevenson, is used by kind permission of SPCK, London.

The English translation of an extract from the Hutterite Chronicle (1525), copyright G. H. Williams, is used by kind permission of Westminster/ John Knox Press, Louisville KY and SCM Press, London.

Extracts from the *Church Book of St. Andrew's Street Baptist Church, Cambridge* in the edition by K. Parsons (1991) are used by kind permission of the Baptist Historical Society.

Introduction
Reflections on the Water

There are many books written in order to advocate the rightness of baptizing only Christian believers, or to put arguments for and against the
baptism of very young infants. This is not one of them. Certainly, the
first six contributors are all Baptist ministers, and they gladly affirm that
for them the gracious activity of God and human response to His gift of
salvation is best focused in the baptism of believers, that is, in the baptism of Christian disciples who can make their own profession of faith.
But in fact all denominations of the Christian Church, not just Baptists,
practise the baptism of believers.

There are, for example, a good many Lutheran, Anglican, and Roman
Catholic church buildings in modern times that include a baptistery large
enough for the immersion in water of believers past the age of childhood.[1] The *Alternative Service Book of the Church of England* places its
order of service for 'The baptism and confirmation of adults' ahead of
the order for the baptism of children. The modern Roman Catholic *Rites*
(as authorized by the Second Vatican Council) give a similar placing to
the 'Christian Initiation of Adults' through baptism. As society becomes
more secular, or multicultural, many of those coming into Christian faith
will inevitably be coming within the fellowship of the Church for the first
time, and will be baptized as believers. It may well be that the normal
mode of baptism will soon be as it once was in the early days of the
Church, when it was a minority group in the pre-Christian Roman
Empire.

The contributors to this volume therefore want to prompt all Christians to ask what the act of believers' baptism they practise tells us about
the nature of God and the world. As we *reflect on* the meaning of baptism, what wider realities can be seen *reflected in* these waters? As an
event rooted in the material world and in a human community, which
expresses salvation in Christ and immersion into the very Spirit of God,
baptism will reflect the image of the triune God, and it will reflect aspects of society and nature that are His creations. It is these implications
that the writers want to follow up. They believe that baptism offers a crucial perspective on God, the natural world, the church, social groups, and
politics. The cover of this volume shows a painting by Claude Monet
(*Water Lilies*, 1907) in which the surface of the water reflects earth and
sky; the three elements merge on the water into a visionary light. The

writers hope that the water of baptism may become such a point of seeing how 'all things hold together in Christ.'

Though this is not therefore a polemical volume, the Baptist essayists do believe that the reflections can be best seen when it is believers who are baptized. This underlies each of their essays. They are of course well aware that while all Christian churches baptize believers, Baptists are different from others in *only* baptizing believers. The writers are so enthusiastic about the richness of meaning and experience in believers' baptism, that they are bound to point out that this is why Baptists baptize believers *instead of* children, rather than *in adddition to* children. In this way they hope to make a contribution to the ecumenical debate about baptism through a different strategy from the usual cross-currents of argument about scripture and tradition. They aim in this way also to make a contribution to Baptist identity, not only by explaining themselves to ecumenical partners, but by awakening among Baptists a sense of the treasure that Baptists hold in store for the worldwide Church.

It should already be apparent that the writers place emphasis on the nature of baptism as a *drama*. The opening essay by Roger Hayden therefore provides a short history of the practice of believers' baptism from the angle of describing what happens in the event. His account spans the early Church Fathers, Anabaptists on the Continent of Europe, seventeenth- and eighteenth-century English Baptists, and Baptists in Eastern Europe in the present day. The essay is deliberately a kind of anthology, quoting amply from documents that give firsthand witness of the way that believers' baptism actually takes place in a variety of different communities. Inevitably, since the main contributors to this volume are all English Baptists, the accounts tend to concentrate upon this cultural context. It is especially important, then, to include a piece from a Romanian pastor, representing Baptist life in a country where there are over 1,400 Baptist congregations containing some 109,000 baptized church members, and which after the demise of communism have recently experienced greater freedom in worship and mission. Though from different places and different times, the stories in this opening essay show the way that believers' baptism is a dramatic event, using all the senses, engaging the whole person, and laying stress upon the manifesting of salvation through action as well as word.

The next essay reflects theologically upon the nature of this dramatic activity, both human and divine, with the help of the term 'sacrament'.

Christopher Ellis begins by taking up the historic preference of many Baptists for the word 'ordinance' rather than 'sacrament', as mentioned in the previous chapter. He finds that the suspicion of some Baptists towards the notion that baptism is a sacrament is grounded in a typical Baptist concern to affirm the sovereign freedom of God, who is not to be trapped within any one particular means of grace in granting His salvation. Accepting this, he urges that Baptists can nevertheless use the term 'sacrament' of baptism in a way that exactly points to the freedom of God to work through a plurality of means in our world.

Indeed, he maintains that when baptism is understood as the baptism of believers we are bound to be brought to a view of sacrament in which God's freedom is celebrated, since believers' baptism requires us to recognize that the divine activity of salvation can occur before, during, and after the act of baptism itself. Believers' baptism prompts us to a view of sacrament that embraces such aspects as the presence of God, human proclamation, divine-human partnership, prophecy, and divine promise. But it also enables us to realize that God is beyond the control of the Church, to say 'he is at work here, but not only here.' One dazzling reflection in the water of believers' baptism is the image of a God whose lordship is in His freedom.

The next essay builds on the idea of sacrament in the previous one, affirming that the baptism of believers allows for the fullest expression of an encounter with God through the 'stuff' of the created world. Paul Fiddes reflects on the way that the personal, triune God, who is always present in our world to influence and change human personalities, nevertheless makes himself present in a deeper way through the element of water in baptism. In doing this, Fiddes considers five motifs connected with water that have been important for the Judaeo-Christian tradition: birth, cleansing, conflict, refreshment, and journey. He argues that the event of believers' baptism opens up an expansion of meaning about salvation as it evokes experiences connected with these motifs in everyday life. Thus the baptism of believers does not merely *picture* these central experiences of being in the world; it actually *enables* participation in the creative-redemptive activity of God that is taking place in both the natural world and human community. This in turn has implications for discerning the purpose and the activity of God that He calls disciples of Christ to share.

In the following essay, Brian Haymes takes further the image of 'conflict' that had been identified as one motif in the previous one. To be baptized into Christ is to share the new humanity that God is calling into being, which has ethical consequences that are not only personal but social. Believers' baptism is therefore an event with political significance. In plunging beneath water there is the 'shock' of confrontation with the hostile Powers that spoil life, and the candidate rises to a new life in which the Powers have been disarmed through the resurrection of Christ. In the light of this triumph, oppressive powers are to be resisted and social idols are to be overturned.

What can it mean for the Powers to be defeated, when evil seems to be as strong as ever? Several Christian thinkers have found the decisive victory of Christ to lie in his exposure of the Powers, his 'showing them up' for what they are, so that the spell they cast over people is broken and their reign is fatally undermined. Haymes now relates this insight to the baptism of believers, suggesting that the exposure of the Powers is actualized in the confession of the person being baptized. The witness of the baptismal candidate continues to weaken the Powers as the truth is manifested for all to see. This has implications for the life of the Christian community, for the Powers can only be stripped bare by a community that is really immersed into the reality of the world. So the sectarian spirit of exclusiveness can be no part of the life of the baptized.

The following essay explores further this overcoming of exclusiveness within the baptismal community. Richard Kidd draws upon tools of social analysis to investigate the role that rituals and signs play in the making of cultural identity. Even the sign of baptism can become a means by which a group cuts itself off from others and puts up high boundaries between 'us' and 'them'. Kidd challenges Baptists to notice that there is a danger that the practice of believers' baptism can be a means of putting up a particularly high fence. However, he claims that baptism is in fact a 'living sign', a mark of Christian identity that can come alive in ever-new ways and acquire new meanings in different cultural contexts. It is, as it it were, a 'text' that can be performed in different stages. He suggests that especially the baptism of believers, far from shutting people out, can help to lower the barriers while maintaining a clear Christian identity; the motif of liberation that is vividly expressed within believers' baptism can speak to many situations in our world and enable the Christian community to reach out to the marginalized.

While not losing a grasp on his own firm convictions about believers' baptism, Richard Kidd is pleading for a more 'pluralist' approach to baptism. This is possible because the pluralism he is commending is not the secular kind in which Christ is one option among others, but one in which Christ is always at the centre, whether inside or beyond the church. This is why a community open to others does not lose its identity but gains it.

In the sixth essay, Hazel Sherman picks up the idea expressed in the previous one that baptism is a kind of dramatic 'text' to be performed in different places. Like the first essay, she begins by actually depicting the drama, putting herself in the shoes of candidates waiting—sometimes nervously—for the moment of entering the water. But she relates this drama especially to the central words of the baptismal event, when the candidate is baptized in the name of the Trinity. The affirmation of God as Father, Son, and Spirit is the key 'text to be performed'. The language of Trinity is not a remote speculation, but the way we talk about our experience of a God of superabundance, a God who always breaks boundaries.

The image of a dramatic event also reminds us that through the act of baptism we actually participate in the life of the triune God. We are drawn into the fellowship of Christ in the love of God by the power of the Spirit. Other essayists have also depicted baptism like this, but Sherman explores the implications of sharing in the life of a personal God who creates relationships and calls us into the risky activity of mission. Baptism into the triune name is not a matter of copying God, but participating in God. Believers' baptism is a sharing in the divine pilgrimage, which challenges all ideas of authority and control, and which sharpens our expression of Christian unity.

It should be apparent by now that the first six essays are not separate contributions merely thrown together into a collection. In fact, they were planned together by the six writers as a sequence, and were then discussed and mutually shaped in meetings over a period of six years. This does not mean that all the essayists agree with each other about everything. The essays are still the work of those whose names are attached to them. But none of the essays remained the same after being shared with others, and the writers intended that as a whole they should enable the reader to see the nature of God and the world 'reflected on the water'.

However, this was not the end of the story of the writing of this book. In case the writers should be forming the kind of Baptist 'in-group' about which Richard Kidd warns us in his essay, they invited a non-Baptist who had not been involved in their work to read all the finished essays and reflect upon them. They were delighted that the distinguished New Testament scholar Professor Christopher Rowland agreed to be such a friend and critic, and his own contribution therefore follows as the seventh chapter. He adopts a stance of 'critical solidarity' with the foregoing essays, confessing himself to be 'an erstwhile crypto-Baptist who has never entirely shed these sympathies.' But he raises questions about the nature of the baptized community that he believes need further exploration.

He is, for instance, concerned about the place the child is given in a Christian community that practises believers' baptism. At first, reading this, the reaction of the Baptist contributors was to say that this was the sort of traditional issue about the baptism of children that they had deliberately set on one side. But as they thought about it, they came to realize that it is not possible to talk about the wider issues of God, the world and society without 'placing the child in the midst', and they were grateful for this prompting. In fact, the recent paper issued by the Doctrine and Worship Comittee of the Baptist Union of Great Britain, entitled *Believing and Being Baptized*,[2] makes a point that the contributors would have wanted to develop if they had continued the dialogue further. That is, there is a variety of ways of 'belonging' within the fellowship of the church, and which young children can belong and be given worth without being baptized members. The paper suggests that New Testament metaphors such as body and household of faith can be creatively expanded to express this variety of belonging suitable to the stage of faith and discipleship someone (not just a child) has arrived at. This is an idea about the church that is contained at least in nucleus within the essays of Christopher Ellis on the freedom of God, and that of Richard Kidd about the inclusive nature of community.

One of the contributors, Richard Kidd, makes a brief response to Christopher Rowland on behalf of all. This is not intended to be a riposte, but an attempt to learn from these Anglican reflections, and so to take the thought of the contributors a brief stage further. Kidd is particularly intrigued by Christopher Rowland's urging Baptists to be less apologetic about appearing to be 'sectarian'; Rowland maintains that Baptists should challenge Anglicans to realize that the very act of baptism 'keeps alive the sectarian nature of Christianity', since the person baptized moves dramatically from one kind of allegiance to another. While Rowland argues that 'sectarianism' in the true sense is not exclusivism and separation from the world, Kidd wonders whether we need a new word to describe this new loyalty. The book ends, then, on the note of a dialogue to be continued, a pilgrimage of discovery in which to share.

Finally, by way of introduction, there is something more to be said about the painting of *Water Lilies* by Claude Monet that adorns the cover of this book. For a whole decade in his painting, from 1899 to 1909, Monet concentrated on the surface of the water on the pond that he had dug in his garden at his home in Giverny, which he had planted with water lilies, and into which he had channeled water from the nearby river Epte. In 1909 he exhibited forty-nine canvases of his pond, of which this book cover shows but one. With this exhibition the success that had eluded Monet all his life suddenly came to him; for the first time, people saw the world with his eyes. The surface of the water in a small pond in a garden in a small village in France, a mere fragment of nature, was a focus through which the changing intensity of light in the world could be caught and explored.

This is a good illustration of a sacrament, a small piece of nature in itself, but a focus of the active presence of God as Lord of the whole cosmos. The contributors turn then to the small baptismal pool of the church, to learn how to say 'The earth is the Lord's and all that is in it, the world and those who dwell within it.'

Notes to Introduction

[1]For several examples, see S. Anita Stauffer, *On Baptismal Fonts, Ancient and Modern, Alcuin/GROW Liturgical Study* (Grove Booklets, Bramcote, 1994).

[2]*Believing and Being Baptised. Baptism, So-called Re-baptism and Children in the Church. A Discussion Document from the Doctrine and Worship Committee of the Baptist Union of Great Britain* (BU Publications, London, 1996).

1

Believers Baptized: An Anthology

ROGER HAYDEN

It was at this time that Jesus came from Nazareth in Galilee and was baptized in the Jordan by John. As he was coming up out of the water, he saw the heavens break open and the Spirit descend on him, like a dove. And a voice came from heaven: 'You are my beloved Son; in you I take delight.' At once the Spirit drove him out into the wilderness, and there he remained for forty days tempted by Satan. (Mark 1:9-13)

Baptism has remained a focal point in the life of Christian communities since the Gospels recorded the baptism of Jesus. However, what seemed to be a straightforward incident that marked the beginning of the public ministry of our Lord has turned out to be very controversial in the life of the church. It has never been a simple, clear-cut moment when an inward affirmation of adherence to the Christian faith has been outwardly declared by a disciple.

Baptist historians down the centuries have suggested that the distinctive Baptist witness was always present in the church, illustrating the point from ancient accounts of the rite of believers' baptism, happy to quote evidence, though rarely in context. An example would be the description given by Justin Martyr, in about A.D. 151:

I will explain how we also dedicated ourselves to God when we were made new through Christ . . . As many as are persuaded and believe that the things are true which are taught by us and said to be true, and undertake to be able to live accordingly, are instructed to pray and to entreat God with fasting, for the remission of their past sins, and we pray and fast with them. Then they are brought by us where there is water, and are born again in the same manner in which we were ourselves born again. For, in the name of God, the Father and Lord of the universe, and of our Saviour Jesus Christ, and of the Holy Spirit, they then receive the washing with water . . . there is pronounced in the water over him who has chosen to be born again, and repented of his sins, the name of God the Father and Lord of the universe;

*he who leads to the laver the person that is to be washed calling
Him by this name alone . . . And this washing is called illumina-
tion, because they who learn these things are illuminated in their
understandings. And in the name of Jesus Christ, who was crucified under Pontious Pilate, and in the name of the Holy Ghost,
who through the prophets foretold all things about Jesus, he who
is illuminated is washed.[1]*

However, to suggest that the distinctive 'Baptist' witness has always
been present in the church wherever the primitive rite of believers' baptism has been practised ignores the fact that Baptist Christian congregations are children of the Radical Reformation in the sixteenth century,
with an identifiable community structure in seventeenth century-England.
Anabaptists, or 'Re-baptizers', emerged as distinct communities in
Switzerland, taking the reform doctrines of scripture, grace, and faith to
their logical conclusion for understanding the church as a 'believer-
community'. The following account is of an early Anabaptist meeting in
Switzerland, in January 1525:

*They came to one mind in these things, and in the pure fear of
God they recognized that a person must learn from the divine
Word and preaching a true faith which manifests itself in love,
and receive the true Christian baptism on the basis of the recognized and confessed faith, in the union with God of a true
conscience, [prepared] henceforth to serve God in a holy Christian life with all godliness, also to be steadfast to the end in
tribulation. And it came to pass that they were together until fear
began to come over them, yea, they were pressed in their hearts.
Thereupon, they began to bow their knees to the Most High God
in heaven and called upon him as the Knower of hearts,
implored him to enable them to do his divine will and to manifest
his mercy toward them . . . After the prayer, George Cajacob
arose and asked Conrad [Grebel] to baptize him, for the sake of
God, with the true Christian baptism upon his faith and knowledge. And when he knelt down with that request and desire,
Conrad baptized him, since at that time there was no ordained
deacon to perform such work. After that was done the others similarly desired George to baptize them, which he also did upon*

their request . . . Each confirmed the other in the service of the gospel, and they began to teach and keep the faith.[2]

The unique course taken by the Reformation in England followed the break between King Henry VIII and the See of Rome when his request for a divorce from Queen Katharine was denied. The central place of Scripture was affirmed in the English Church, William Tyndale's translation being primary in the subsequent development of the English Bible. Cranmer's *Book of Common Prayer* was definitive for worship, and *The Thirty-nine Articles* summarized Protestant doctrine. However, as in Switzerland, there were those who felt that reform had not gone far enough. At first there was an attempt to purify doctrine and practice still further along lines advocated in Geneva, but when that failed some believed that the only option was to separate from the Church of England. Puritan and Separatist communities were formed in an attempt to rediscover the lifestyle of the primitive church. Among those communities was a group of Separatists in Gainsborough who, in the face of persecution from the Elizabethan authorities, fled to Holland in 1608.

While in Holland this congregation sought to create a 'true church' whose belief and practice seemed to them, in the light of their understanding of Scripture evidence, to conform strictly to Scripture. John Smyth, an ordained Anglican priest, first baptized himself by affusion, then the rest of the congregation, with the result that the first English Baptist church was formed on Dutch soil. Eventually some of the congregation returned to Spitalfields, London, and in 1611 under the leadership of Thomas Helwys formed themselves into a distinct Arminian, believer-church community known as the General Baptists.

Meanwhile, various Separatist communities in England, whose lifestyle was based upon the theology and model of the church inaugurated by John Calvin in Geneva, came to the conclusion that infant baptism was impossible in the light of their understanding of the church as a believer community and adopted believers' baptism. These Calvinist congregations, with their deep Puritan convictions about the sovereign grace of God in election, were called Particular Baptist churches (from 1638). They were the dominant group among the English Baptists, as Particular and General Baptists pursued their own distinctive theology and patterns of being the church, until they joined in the Baptist Union of Great Britain in 1891.

These Baptist churches were part of classical English Dissent, along with Presbyterians and Congregationalists, who after Cromwell's Commonwealth were branded together as the 'nonconformist' churches in Restoration England. The total separation of church and state was distinctive of their common life, and they were effectively an alternative Christian society in Protestant England. From their earliest days Baptists issued 'Confessions of Faith', which after 1677 tended to take the style of the *Westminster Confession*; these were primarily to express their Christian orthodoxy as well as their essential differences in doctrine and polity. Particular and General Baptist *Confessions* made Scripture determinative for the faith and practice of the churches and thereby affirmed the church to be a believer community that was entered by believers' baptism and where the Christian life was sustained by regular worship at the Lord's Table. Baptists preferred the word 'ordinance' rather than 'sacrament' when describing these things.

The General Baptist *Orthodox Creed*, 1679, provides a detailed paragraph about baptism, in contrast to the brevity of a similar paragraph from the Particular Baptists:

Baptism is an ordinance of the new testament, ordained by Jesus Christ, to be unto the party baptized, or dipped, a sign of our entrance into the covenant of grace, and ingrafting into Christ, and into the body of Christ, which is his church; and of remission of sin in the blood of Christ, and of our fellowship with Christ, in his death and resurrection, and of our living, or rising to newness of life. And orderly none ought to be admitted to the visible church of Christ without first being baptized; and those which do really profess repentance towards God, and faith in, and obedience to our Lord Jesus Christ, are the onely proper subjects of this ordinance, according to our Lord's holy institution, and primitive practice; and ought, by the minister or administrator, to be done in a solemn manner in the name of the father, son and holy ghost, by the immersion or dipping of the person in the element of water; this being necessary due to the administration of this holy sacrament, as holy scripture sheweth and first and best antiquity witnesseth for some centuries of years. But the Popish doctrine which they teach and believe, that those infants which die without baptism, or have it not actually, or in desire, are not, nor cannot be saved, we do not believe. Nor yet their practice of admitting persons only upon an implicit faith of the church, nor their popish ceremonies of salt, and spittle, and breathing on the face of the party baptized, together with their chrisoms and hallowed lights. Neither do we believe that infants dying in infancy without baptism, go to purgatory or limbus infantum, as they erroneously teach. Nor do we believe that the Pope of Rome, or any other person whomsoever, have power to alter, or change, this ordinance of Christ, as they have done by this superstitious, and such like idolatrous inventions and practices of the Romish church. All which superstitions of theirs, are contrary to Christ's institution, or the apostles practice of holy baptism.[3]

When, in the eighteenth century, Methodism emerged as a result of the Evangelical Revival led by the Arminian John Wesley, it was viewed with almost equal suspicion by Dissenters as it was by the Church of England. Dissent, rooted firmly in historic, Calvinistic puritanism, was not at first enamoured of the Revival. It was the Calvinistic aspect of the Revival under George Whitefield which brought new life to Particular Baptist churches.

A Baptist church in Cambridge, with its able pastor, Robert Robinson, who had been converted under Whitefield, could hold its own in the University town. The Church Book for 10 December 1761 carries the following entry by Robert Robinson, as men and women were considered for membership of the church:

This day Robert Silk, Miss Gifford and others were admitted members. The manner of the admission follows. R. Silk, having given notice of his design to the pastor, who had conversed with them in private, attended. The pastor stood at the head of the [communion] table; the deacons next him on each side, and the members in the table and adjoining pews: sitting. The pastor began by a short discourse on the nature of Christ's kingdom, qualifications of his subjects, etc, and closed by proposing R. Silk to them for fellow-citizen. Then he spent a few minutes in prayer. Silk, who stood at the bottom of the table-seat . . . was asked to speak as in the presence of God the truth only. He was told that

*faith and repentance were the two prerequisites to church-fellow-
ship. The first he was desired to speak: the last, he was told,
would be inquired in his life . . . The man then gave an account
of his former profane life, and of his late change, declaring his
faith in the Gospel of Christ. When he was ended he was desired
to withdraw.*

*In Silk's absence the pastor recapitulated what had been said by
R. Silk, and observed, that though a profession of faith in Christ
was necessary to church fellowship: though the practice was
clearly apostolical: though the custom of this church, and others
of the same discipline, was preferable to the customs of those
churches, which either on the one hand required nothing but a
decent conduct, and sometimes not that; or on the other, imposed
creeds on their members to subscribe; not suffering people to express their own ideas in their own language: though this church,
like the churches of the first 300 years after Christ, required
those that were to be baptized to renounce the devil and all his
works, and to declare their faith in Christian truths; yet after all,
he said, we ought not to forget that this, with every other institution, is subject to gross abuses and fallacies. He said, that all
men showed themselves to others by their bright sides; that the
temptation to do it in this case was that all a man said about his
own experience was in reality no more than the man's opinion
of himself; that if men were subject to partiality, it was when
they judged their own cause: that all the man had said might be
true, for it was not impossible: it might also be false, for some
men are capable of anything. He said there were two things
extremely important. One was whether his moral conduct was
upright, for that proved the goodness of faith, and such a member would be an honour to any society in the world; and the
other was whether his temper was captious and litigious: free
from that he would be a son of peace in the church. He added,
the man is withdrawn to give room for free debate. The members
approved what he had said; and his neighbours spoke well of his
life. He was then recalled. The pastor inquired what he thought
of baptism. He desired it by immersion. The Covenant was read,
and he was asked whether he would make that his rule of*

conduct to us. He agreed. He was then told that the pastor would inquire his character, and if that were good, fix a day to baptize him. The pastor prayed and dismissed the assembly. This was the last church meeting. In the interim his character had been inquired, he had been baptized, and was now presented to the church again. The pastor asked whether the church was willing to receive him. They voted by holding up their hands. The pastor then took him by the hand and said, 'I give you the right hand of fellowship; a token of full communion with this church of Christ.'[4]

A few years later, in 1767, when there was an unusual day of baptizing shared between the Cambridge and the Saffron Walden Baptist churches, Robinson recorded the proceedings of the joint open-air baptismal service held at Whittlesford, in a mill pond:

This day the two churches of Walden and Cambridge met by mutual consent at Whittlesford to administer the ordinance of baptism. This church sometimes administers baptism in public (as now) in the presence of many hundred spectators; so John the Baptist administered it; sometimes in private; so S. Paul administered it to the jailor; though never in the night, because we are not only not persecuted, but we are protected by law. Circumstances must determine when a private, or when a public baptism is proper. Previous to this, twenty-five persons had professed their faith and repentance to the church at Walden; and twenty-one had done the same at Cambridge; and all had desired baptism by immersion. Dr. Gifford, at ten o'clock, mounted a moveable pulpit near the river in Mr Hollick's yard, and, after singing and prayer, preached a suitable sermon on the occasion from Psalm cxix.57. After sermon, the men retired to one room, the women to two others, and the baptizer, Mr Gwennap, to another, to prepare for the administration. After about half an hour, Mr Gwennap, dressed as usual (except a coat, which was supplied by a black gown made like a bachelor's) came down to the waterside. He was followed by the men, two and two, dressed as usual, only, instead of a coat, each one had on a long white blaize gown, tied round the waist with a piece of worstead-

binding, and leaded at the bottom that they might sink; they had on their heads white linen caps. The women followed, two and two, dressed as usual, only all had white gowns, holland or dimitty. Their upper-coats were tacked to their stockings, and their gown leaded, lest their clothes should float. Mr Gwennap sang a hymn at the waterside, spoke about 10 minutes on the subject, and then taking the oldest man of the company by the hand, led him to a convenient depth in the river. Then pronouncing the words, I baptize thee in the name of the Father, of the Son, and of the Holy Ghost, he immersed the person once in the river. Robinson stood in a boat, and, with other assistants, led the rest in, and, having wiped their faces after their baptism, led them out. Mr Gwennap added a few words after the administration at the water-side, and concluded with the usual blessing.[5]

Although distinctly eighteenth century in its style, Robert Robinson's account still catches the mood of many Baptist congregations today in both their concerns and witness. Conversion is perceived as the beginning of the Christian life. Nurture in the family of the church and education by participation in worship where the Scripture is read and preached are vital preparations for becoming a Christian; but no one is, or should be, called a Christian until there has been a personal encounter with God through Jesus Christ. It is the personal acceptance of God's grace in salvation through trust in Jesus Christ by which a person is born again, which undergirds the true life of the church.

Accounts of believers' baptism in the present day continue to demonstrate the deep sense of personal commitment that runs through every person's experience as he or she accepts the discipline of obedience to Christ in baptism. In recent years Baptists have been concerned with the meaningful presentation of Christian faith to those who have learning difficulties, for whom the drama of the event speaks clearly of a commitment that their disability makes it difficult for them to put into words. Yet their faith is real, and their joy in Christ infectious. In March 1990, Richard Bowers, who has Down's Syndrome, was baptized at Central Baptist Church in Bloomsbury, London. His immediate family and his wider family of the congregation shared in his commitment. A few years later he was asked to contribute something for an ecumenical meeting on the subject 'What I like about the church', and he chose to speak about his baptism, dictating an account of what had happened and what it had meant for him, which was later also published in the church magazine:

> *Bloomsbury Central Baptist Church is a very nice place. I was baptized there four years ago, when I became like a Christian. My family all came to the worship of the church. Howard Williams and Barbara and Maurice Johns were there. I wore special clothes—white shirt and cream trousers and just feet. Maurice Johns led Barbara into the water—it was open. Then he took me to the baptismal water. I go down the steps. Barbara was preaching. My hands together on my tummy. Barbara said: 'Father, Son and Holy Spirit take me' and I was baptized. Barbara tip me over under the water. My brother came in the water and helped me, wrapped me up to keep me warm. I changed my clothes. Afterwards all my family in the porch in the front of the church—my father took photographs. Then we come back downstairs and everyone helped celebrate of me—with nice cards and presents. I am a member of the church. I like the communion service. I wear a little cross to show I am a Christian.*[6]

The depth of faith and ongoing commitment show through this dictated report despite, or perhaps even because, of the language difficulty; it makes a moving testimony to the power of the act of baptism itself.

In a different cultural setting, a baptism took place recently at Ferentari Baptist Church in Bucharest, Romania, and the pastor of the church gave this account of how a nineteen-year-old girl came to baptism.

> *Maria was nineteen and worked in a factory as a seamstress. A friend at work, Monica, had invited her to attend the Baptist church in which she was a member, and in time Maria herself had come to request baptism as a Christian believer. A strong influence in bringing her to this moment of faith was the friendship of the many young people in the church. The baptismal class, which the church calls Catechism, lasted for three months. During one and a half hours each Sunday morning, the 24 people who wanted to be baptized were given basic bible teaching and also instructed in what Baptists believe. Each was given a Baptist Confession of Faith and they were encouraged to study it*

together with the Bible. Maria learned about the importance of participating in the life of the church as a member.

When the date for the baptism was decided, all the candidates were invited to meet with the church committee, that is the elders and the deacons. The candidates had to give an account of their experience of conversion to Christ, and what had changed in their lives following that point. What Maria and most of the other candidates were really scared about were the 'doctrinal questions', when each of them had to respond to a question from the Confession of Faith. But the elders encouraged Maria, affirmed her Christian commitment and accepted her for baptism. She was given a white robe for baptism on the next Sunday morning, but meanwhile she was invited to the midweek meeting to give a 'testimony' in front of the whole church. All the candidates found this a joyous service, and Maria walked home feeling she was part of the church family.

On Sunday morning the candidates were there early in church, all dressed in white robes. There was a photographic session before the service began so that members of the family and of the church could have memories of the event before the robes became wet. The church was packed with more than three hundred people. As soon as the pastor said 'Amen' at the end of his sermon, the candidates sang 'I have decided to follow Jesus', and then Maria was the first to enter the baptismal pool. The pastor said, 'Sister Maria, in front of this cloud of seen and unseen witnesses, I ask you if you believe in Jesus Christ as your Lord and Saviour?' She replied 'yes', and he asked again, 'Do you promise to obey and follow him till the end of your life?' 'Yes', she responded, and the pastor raised his hand and declared: 'Based on your testimony and at the command of our Lord Jesus Christ I baptize you in the name of the Father, the Son and the Holy Spirit'. The pastor dipped Maria beneath the water, and as she came out of the pool the choir sang, 'Those who have been baptized in Christ have also risen in Christ.' Maria found that she was shaking with emotion.

After all the candidates were baptized they changed quickly and came to the front of the congregation where the elders prayed for each of them and laid hands on them. Following the benediction they went out to be greeted by the pastor and the people with the usual word of greeting, 'Pace' (peace), and to receive flowers. Now Maria was a member of the church, and next Sunday she would take communion for the first time.[7]

These two very different accounts, from London and Bucharest, are united by their common understanding of baptism as a person-centred event, not only for the candidate but for the congregation and all who witness it.

Like all Christian communities, Baptists have strengths and weaknesses, and the recognition of these is important for their well-being and further development. In the past Baptists have often felt that their argument with other Christians was concerned with the *mode* of baptism: that it must be by total immersion in water as well as in the name of the triune God. Subsequently and inevitably, the discussion then centred upon whether the person being baptized had a personal faith in Christ as Lord and Saviour. In any discussion of baptism, Baptists regard conversion as fundamental, with the result that baptism has often been regarded predominantly—but never entirely—as an outward and visible declaration, a public witness. In the 1960s, under the influence of liturgical renewal, British Baptists reflected theologically upon the nature of baptism as a sign of God's covenant of grace, and particularly its vital relationship to reception into membership of the church, universal and local. The extent to which that insight was grasped is seen in the growing acceptance that a service of baptism should conclude with the reception of the new convert into membership of the church by laying on of hands and participation in the Lord's Supper. This single liturgical act is now current practice for many Baptist congregations, bringing a new depth to the Baptist understanding of the multi-faceted jewel that is baptism. In so doing, however, it has revealed the weakness of much previous discussion, which was too narrowly concerned with the mode of baptism as mainly a means of public witness.

The definitive study by the Baptist New Testament scholar George R. Beasley-Murray, *Baptism in the New Testament*,[8] presented the exegesis and theology of the New Testament uncontrolled by the traditions of the separated denominations, and this has found wide acceptance in scholarly circles. Baptists generally feel that the argument from New Testament evidence about believers' baptism has been won, whatever might be the view on the developing tradition in the church. In a postscript Beasley-Murray made suggestions by which the ecumenical dilemma could be addressed by Baptist and other Christian denominations. On the one hand, he urged paedo-Baptist churches to reexamine the practice of 'indiscriminate baptism' outside the context of Christian families and to 'increase the number of baptisms of believers of responsible age in the ordinary services of the churches'.[9] On the other hand, he urged Baptist churches to 'refrain from requesting the baptism of those baptized in infancy who wish to join our churches, and to administer baptism to such only where there is a strong appeal for it from the applicant.'[10] He noted that this was actually in line with the practice of 'open membership' Baptist churches in England, but that it was a challenging idea for some other Baptist Unions in other parts of the world.

Much has happened in British church life since those words were written. The ecumenical experiments at local level between congregations already in existence and the formation of single ecumenical congregations with a shared building have brought a deeper awareness of the baptismal issue. Methodists have worked hard with Baptists to produce a national concordat on baptismal policy that gives liberty of conscience a pastoral place in ecumenical congregations. As yet there is no similar agreement with other mainstream ecumenical partners, although in 1996 formal talks are well-advanced between the Baptist Union and the United Reformed Church, and discussions with the Church of England are in process, which are attempting to resolve the issue of so-called 'second baptism'.

Through all these important conversations the stories remain of believers baptized; stories of Justin, Conrad Grebel, Richard Silk, the twenty-five believers at Saffron Walden, Richard Bowers, Maria. They also provide the narrative framework in which these present essays attempt to speak about baptism in a different way from the usual ecumenical debate. We aim to place baptism in the context not only of the church but also of the wider society and the natural world, and we believe that this could prove creative, not just for Baptists, but for the whole Church of Christ.

Notes to Chapter 1

[1]Justin Martyr, *Apology for the Christians I*, 61-7: translated in J. Stevenson (Ed.), *A New Eusebius. Documents Illustrative of the History of the Church to A.D. 337* (SPCK, London, 1957), pp. 65-66.

[2]Excerpt from the Hutterite Chronicle (1525), translated in G. H. Williams and A. M. Mergal (Eds.), *Spiritual and Anabaptist Writers. Documents Illustrative of the Radical Reformation*. The Library of Christian Classics. Ichthus Edition (Westminster Press, Philadelphia, 1957), pp. 43-44.

[3]W. L. Lumpkin, *Baptist Confessions of Faith*, (Judson Press, Philadelphia, 1969), pp. 317-318; cf. p. 167.

[4]K. A. C. Parsons (Ed.), *Church Book: St Andrews' Street Baptist Church, Cambridge, 1720-1832* (Baptist Historical Society, London, 1991), pp. 29f.

[5]Ibid., pp. 41-42.

[6]Richard Bowers has given permission for this account to be published here.

[7]Personal letter from the Revd Otniel Bunaciu to the editor, October 1995.

[8]G. R. Beasley-Murray, *Baptism in the New Testament* (Macmillan, London, 1963).

[9]Ibid., pp. 388-89.

[10]Ibid., p. 392.

2

Baptism and the
Sacramental Freedom of God

CHRISTOPHER ELLIS

It may come as a surprise to many Christians that most Baptists do not refer to baptism as a sacrament. But then it may also surprise some that Baptists have a wide range of views about baptism altogether. There is certainly a core of agreement, especially about the need for the person being baptized to have faith and the importance, though not absolute necessity, of immersion.[1] Thus, all Baptists can agree that, as well as the rite symbolizing the forgiveness of sins, the person being baptized is following the example of Jesus Christ, submitting to the command of the risen Christ, and confessing his or her own personal faith in Christ. The differences begin when it is asked: 'What does *God* do in baptism?' There will be those who wish to see in the rite only a God-given vehicle for the response of faith. Others will claim that God is able to use the 'experience' of baptism just as He may use other parts of worship, such as the preaching of the Word. Yet others will want to say that something has 'happened' in baptism through the grace of God, and that things are different afterwards from what they were before.

Baptists, together with other baptistic groups, offer a minority yet significant witness within the church as a whole. This distinctive, or disruptive, voice speaks out because of a belief in what baptism should be that is at variance with the larger part of the world church. Such disruption needs to be explained to others and examined by Baptists themselves. Others need to understand some of the concerns that are focused in this commitment to the baptism of believers. At the same time, Baptists need to question whether the battles of the past are still relevant, and to ask if there are places where ground may be shared without a sacrifice of basic principles. This presents a challenge both to other Christians about the coherence of their own baptismal theology and to Baptists, who have much to gain by entering into a richer theological inheritance concerning the meaning of believers' baptism.

Traditionally, Baptists have preferred the word *ordinance* to the word *sacrament*. The word 'ordinance' side-stepped the issue of sacramental theology by placing the importance of the rite in the believer's and the church's obedience to the command of Christ.[2] However, the word 'sacrament' has often been rejected because of assumptions about what others have been thought to believe about sacraments, rather than because there is no sacramental element in Baptist thinking about baptism. Here an attempt is made to give meaning to a Baptist use of the word 'sacrament' with regard to baptism.

Freedom has been an important theme for Baptists since the beginning of the seventeenth century. It was not only a concern that Baptists might be free to worship but that others, including people of other faiths, should be free in this regard.[3] But freedom needs to be developed not only in our concern for human freedom but in our recognition of the nature of divine activity. In baptismal terms this directs us to a recognition of the sovereignty of the Spirit in liturgy as well as life, and enables us to affirm the activity of God within a sacramental action while denying His enslavement within an automatic process.

1. Sacramental themes

This is not the place for a study of the development of sacramental theology in the wider church, whether East or West, but there is an important matter of method that needs to be acknowledged.[4] The word 'sacrament' may well be important for indicating a richness of theological understanding of baptism, but to define the word sacrament itself as the key for interpretation would be to offer an abstract filter through which much goodness might be lost. However, the underlying concerns of sacramental theology need to be recognized and will offer signposts for our examination of believers' baptism.[5]

It is arguably more important to *expound* the meaning of the sacraments than define them. What truths are being expressed, what traces of divine activity, what dynamics of the gospel are encountered here?

(i) Continuing incarnation

Sacramental theology begins with the symbolism of water, bread, and wine. The explanation of what is involved cannot avoid the use of the material as sign and symbol. Augustine's *signum* and the *Book of Common Prayer*'s 'outward visible sign of an inward spiritual grace' both express the embodiedness of the sacraments.[6] This is directly linked to the Incarnation of Christ, the embodied nature of discipleship whereby the church is called to live in the world, and the eschatological hope whereby the sacramental use of material things might prefigure the redemption of all things. Here is a link between creation and redemption, where the experience of God using water, bread, and wine provides a lens for seeing the world and God's activity in a new light.

(ii) The activity of God

What does God do in baptism? In a famous sermon in the middle of the nineteenth century, John Keble claimed, 'Once a child is baptized he is a Christian forever unless by his own sin he casts away the grace granted him'.[7] By contrast, some Baptist expositions so stress baptism as a human response to God's grace that it seems nothing is said about what God is doing. Other Baptists are able to speak of baptism as a means of grace but emphasize that such grace is totally dependent on the faith of the recipient. So, also in the nineteenth century, the Baptist writer J. M. Cramp observed in the development of baptismal theology what he called unscriptural opinions: 'A notion had grown up, that baptism actually accomplished what was professed in it'.[8] An affirmation about the activity of God brings with it questions concerning *what* God does in baptism, *when* He does it, and *how*. These are not pedantic or even unseemly questions, for they have divided Christians for hundreds of years. The traditional answers have often been the places from which Baptists have run, but we still have to face the questions.

(iii) The promises of God

Part of the pastoral pressure that led to developments in baptismal theology arose from the need for assurance. A stress upon Dominical institution, and belief in divine activity leading to the claim of efficacy *ex opere operato*, can be seen as mechanisms that offer assurance to the anxious recipient in a dangerous world.[9] It can be argued that an emphasis on God's promise rather than activity might enable a more holistic approach to what is happening in baptism, an approach that encompasses not only divine initiative but divinely inspired human response.

(iv) Human response

While the dynamics of assurance might play down the part of human
faith in baptism, it is still a significant theme, and for Baptists it is crucial. There may be disagreement about whose faith needs to be exercised
—whether that of the person being baptized, the sponsors, or the church.
That is another debate. The point here is that a human response is
needed, and a proper acknowledgement of the work of the Spirit will recognize that even a so-called human response is a gift of grace and an
activity that takes place within the life of God.[10]

(v) Sacraments and the church

One of the benefits of the modern Liturgical Movement has been to bring
the sacraments into the centre of the church's life. For those practising
infant baptism this has meant infants being presented in the main services, and for Baptists there has been an increased emphasis on the link
between baptism and church membership. There are three parties in the
sacramental partnership: God, the person being baptized, and the people
of God. This recognition encourages an acknowledgement of the function
of the sacraments within the life of the church. Thus baptism is both a
celebration of the faith of the people of God and a means of grace
whereby the church is challenged to be a sacramental sign of the Kingdom of God.

(vi) A focus of salvation

The emphasis on God acting in a gracious and saving way in baptism is
related to a recognition that both baptism and the Eucharist embody the
gospel. In baptism the forgiveness of sins is demonstrated, union with
Christ in his death and resurrection affirmed, the gift of the Spirit
claimed, and membership of the church realized locally. Whether divine
grace or human response is emphasized, the gospel of Christ is
proclaimed.

(vii) The centrality of Jesus Christ

The centrality of Christ is clear in baptism and communion, not only because they are believed to be instituted by him, but also because they bear eloquent witness to what God has done in Christ and what He seeks to do through the body of Christ. This is crucial to our understanding of the sacraments. The story and words of Jesus provide a narrative framework for the enacted symbolism of washing, eating, and drinking. Baptists have used the word *ordinance* to indicate that what the church does, it does in obedience to its Lord.

In baptism the one to be baptized is seen to be following the example of Christ, and yet this is an inadequate explanation. The person moves beyond following an example to being united with the risen Christ in the power of the Spirit—united with Christ in his baptism, in his death on the cross, and in his resurrection. Thus the believer rises from the water to live the resurrection life in the 'inbetween time', between the ascension of Christ and his final coming in glory. Baptism gains its shape from the story of Jesus and its promise and challenge from the union with Christ of the believer who continues to live in the world that crucified Jesus.

2. Baptist concerns

It is no easy task to present Baptist teaching on baptism. As already indicated, there is a wide spectrum of interpretation about the meaning of the rite, and a survey of Baptist writings on baptism will show that many contributors have been concerned with polemical issues over and against the rest of the Christian church. They have been primarily concerned with *who* is a proper subject of baptism—i.e. a believer as opposed to an infant—and the *method* of baptism—i.e. baptism by immersion rather than sprinkling. These emphases may be understandable, but they have impoverished Baptists. They reduce the possibility of a rich Baptist affirmation about the nature and meaning of baptism and short-change the rest of the church that consequently suffers from this lack of Baptist witness. Nonetheless, it is possible to draw together a number of strands that can show the areas of Baptist concern.

(i) Submission to Scripture

The early Baptists grew out of the radical, Separatist strand of the Reformation. The rallying cry of *sola scriptura* was viewed with a thorough-going seriousness, and it was their reading of the New Testament with regard to the church that led the Separatists to break away from the state church. It was a similar searching of the Scriptures with regard to baptism that led Separatists who had emigrated to Amsterdam under John Smyth and Thomas Helwys in 1608 to embrace believers' baptism and provide the beginnings of the General Baptists. Similarly, the Particular Baptists emerged in the 1630s as a group of Calvinistic Separatists who removed themselves from other Calvinists because of their reading of the New Testament with regard to baptism. This overall emphasis remains: Baptists will want all theological claims to be tested by Scripture alone.

This radical position has meant that debates with Paedo-Baptists have often been fruitless because the parties have played by different rules. The question can be posed in a way that will sharpen awareness as Baptist reactions to the development of sacramental theology are examined. Are Baptists prepared to allow for a development of practice and theology in the developing life of the church beyond New Testament days, provided those developments express truths that can be attested as scriptural truths?[11]

(ii) A believers' church

Fundamental to any Baptist teaching is a view of the church as the fellowship of believers. This Separatist emphasis developed from their reading of the New Testament account of the beginnings of the church and its teaching about the nature and purpose of the people of God. From this belief flows the ordering of local churches with membership and church meetings, the Reformation emphasis on faith, and the evangelical emphasis on 'experimental religion'. Thus the understanding of the church cannot be separated from discussion about the nature of baptism, not only with regard to initiation but also with regard to the relationship of grace and faith.

(iii) Baptism is the baptism of believers

The most obvious testimony that separates Baptists from the majority of the wider church is that baptism is for believers, but it must not be separated from the Baptist understanding of the church. Believers' baptism will place high on the agenda the role of the Spirit in baptism but need not assume a priority of faith over grace. Indeed, remembering that the majority of Baptist churches today have developed from the 'Particular' —or Calvinistic—stream, a very high place must be given to the gracious activity of God. The issue for Baptists is not whether grace has priority, but the kind action of grace within baptism itself.

(iv) Baptism by immersion is the norm

The Particular Baptist Confession of 1644 states:

> The way and manner of the dispensing of the Ordinance the Scripture holds out to be dipping or plunging the whole body under water; it being a signe, must answer the thing signified, which are these: first, the washing of the whole soule in the bloud of Christ: Secondly, that interest the Saints have in the death, buriall, and resurrection: thirdly, together with a confirmation of our faith, that as certainly as the body is buried under water, and riseth againe, so certainly shall the bodies of the Saints be raised by the power of Christ in the body of the resurrection, to reigne with Christ.[12]

It is important to note that immersion emerged as an issue only some years after the conviction about believers' baptism. While Baptists have affirmed the potency of immersion as a powerful symbol and as the likely interpretation of *baptizo*, it is not as important as the faith of the person being baptized. Many Baptists, for pastoral and other reasons, have acknowledged that immersion in water is the norm rather than the absolute rule.[13]

(v) Suspicion of sacramentalism

It is vital that we try to understand the context within which the negative attitude towards sacramentalism developed within Baptist teaching. The trajectory of the radical Reformation that led to the Separatists in general and the Baptists in particular was partly governed by a reading of the New Testament reading that resulted in a 'gathered church', and partly by the belief that the Roman church and some of the Reformed churches were wrong in their institutional commitment to a comprehensive 'state' church. As victims of persecution, they saw how the sacramental structures could be used as instruments of manipulation and control. The *ex opere operato* theologies objectified divine activity within the institutional processes of liturgical activity, thus enabling church and state to control the dispensing of salvation.

The positive implication of this Baptist reaction was to affirm a God beyond the control of the church. The sovereignty of God is a vital theological perspective in any debate concerning the locus of divine activity within the sacraments. Here faith becomes important for another reason than those given previously. God is to be in control: the right words and the right actions are not enough; otherwise the correct formulae would lead to divine activity being turned on and off as a tap. The importance of faith is the recognition that faith involves trust and reliance upon the grace of God. Therefore, if faith becomes the key pivot of divine activity, that very faith looks to God's graciousness and offers not an anthropocentric but theocentric understanding of what happens in baptism.[14]

Alongside fears about domesticating grace within the sacraments, later Baptists were also concerned about the appropriateness of what was being claimed about what baptism achieved. The reaction amongst British Baptists against sacramental theology and language in the nineteenth and early twentieth century was largely a reaction against the influence of the Oxford Movement. Baptists such as C. H. Spurgeon urged that the focus of salvation was in relation to Jesus Christ, not submission to the sacramental mechanisms of the church.[15]

(vi) Salvation and union with the body of Christ

A further observation needs to be made about the locus of divine activity. Believers' baptism assumes faith on the part of the one being baptized *prior* to the baptism. No distinction can be made between saving faith and any other kind of faith. Therefore, the logic of the Baptist position must lead to the recognition that salvation has not only been offered, but accepted before the baptism takes place. The two primary strands woven together in the present Baptist denomination are the Particular, or

Calvinistic, Baptists from the seventeenth century and the General Baptists of the New Connexion who arose out of the Evangelical Revival of the eighteenth century. Calvinists will already have located salvation in the election of the saints or the working of prevenient grace. Those from within the Arminian, evangelical stream will identify the faith of the believer as evidence of the accepting of God's gracious forgiveness in Christ. In either case, faith is undergirded by a theology that identifies saving faith as present and active prior to the presenting of the candidate for baptism.

If this chronological, yet theological, claim is accepted, then it leads to a development of some importance. Much of the debate about the activity of God in baptism has been focused on the assumption that this activity involves the granting of salvation for the first time. However, the existence of faith prior to baptism offers two approaches, both of which exclude the possibility of baptism as the initial means to salvation. On the one hand, those who wish to make a sharp distinction between justification and sanctification must accept that the existence of faith indicates the activity of the Spirit and the active response of the believer prior to the moment of baptism. On the other hand, this prior reality of faith can encourage us to view salvation as a process within which baptism plays a significant part. Baptism may be seen as a medium of the Spirit who has already impinged on the person and led him or her to a confession of faith and a life of discipleship. Now the symbolism of water, burial, and resurrection; the invoking of the triune Name; and the partnership of the people of God all lead to a new stage of life in the Spirit, in union with Christ and amongst the company of his people.

The church cannot be excluded from any interpretation of God's activity in salvation. One objective aspect of baptism is the making visible of the incorporation of the believer into the body of Christ. This is a moment when the divine activity may be seen, in part, as the process whereby the individual believer, expressing personal faith in Christ, is made a member of the local community of God's people. This initiation is more than a social action undertaken by the local church, because it arises out of the union of the believer with the crucified, buried, and raised Christ who is head of the church.

(vii) Unease with ritual

Over the years Baptists have tended to pride themselves on what they often call their 'simple' worship. What this usually means, unfortunately, is not *simple* but *abstract* worship. The early Separatists were very suspicious of anything that might smack of 'popery', and that suspicion has influenced Baptist worship ever since. Horton Davies claims that Baptists went further than other Separatists in their opposition to set forms of worship.[16] John Smyth, a Baptist founding father, asserted:

> That the reading out of a Book is no part of spiritual worship, but the invention of the man of sin; that Books and writings are in the nature of Pictures and Images; that it is unlawful to have the Book before the eyes in singing of a Psalm.[17]

A contemporary description of worship in the Amsterdam fellowship suggests that even Bibles were put aside when it came to a time of 'spiritual' worship, although the Particular Baptists were closer to the other Separatists in their forms of worship.[18]

When we place this heritage alongside an emphasis on personal faith and 'experimental religion', we can see that even believers' baptism—which distinguished Baptists from other Christians—has had to be viewed through a lens that views actions in worship as unimportant and ritual as suspect. Yet the diversity of Baptist life must never be ignored. This diversity is not only to be found between different positions, but within the tension experienced by individual exponents. For example, the emphasis on immersion (while not absolute) was not only based in obedience to the New Testament but inevitably led to the conclusion that the action should signify what is being expressed, i.e. burial with Christ.[19]

(viii) Symbol or sacrament?

Many Baptists have had a considerable uneasiness about sacramental language. Whilst it is inaccurate to use 'ordinance' as an alternative, non-sacramental designation for baptism and the Eucharist, the very misuse of the word points to a reality within denominational life.

Those Baptist scholars who have produced substantial biblical studies on baptism have tended to remind Baptists uneasy about sacraments of the theocentric emphasis of Scripture.[20] The committee that reported to the Baptist Union Council in 1937 concerning a possible union with Congregationalists and Presbyterians was able to speak of baptism as 'a means of grace' and urged Baptists to reconsider sympathetically 'a more sacramental, i.e. Calvinistic, view of both baptism and the Lord's Supper'.[21]

John Gill, an eighteenth-century Baptist scholar, held a view of baptism highly centred upon the individual, which included the washing away of sin, the remission of sins, and the representing of the sufferings, burial, and resurrection of Christ. Yet these meanings are described as the 'ends and uses' of baptism that suggest a closer connection between action and meaning than that of mere representation. Indeed, Andrew Fuller in his circular letter of 1802 to the Northampton Association claimed:

> Sin is washed away in baptism in the same sense as Christ's flesh is eaten, and his blood drunk, in the Lord's Supper: the sign, when rightly used, leads to the thing signified.

We must admit that there is considerable diversity among Baptists concerning how baptism is a means of grace. Both the Orthodox General Baptist Confession of 1678 and the Particular Baptist Confession of 1689 agree that baptism is a sign of the believer's fellowship with Christ in his death and resurrection, of being ingrafted in his body, of the remission of sin, and of the newness of life. But what is a sign? How can the action of grace in baptism be described? What is the relationship between any *objective* interpretation of baptism and the inevitable *subjective* effect on the recipient? These are questions to which we must return.

(ix) The freedom of God

A number of times in this discussion we have recognized that the debate concerning the activity of God is largely to do with placing it within, before, or beyond the action of baptism itself. Part of the problem has been the assumption that there is one correct answer to the question; yet if we look at the New Testament we find a very different picture.

The book of Acts testifies to the untidiness of the Holy Spirit. The Spirit is given *before* baptism in the case of Cornelius and *after* in the case of the Samaritans evangelized by Philip.[22] On occasion, evidence of the Spirit is used as a nudge to the developing church to transcend barriers that might be in danger of imprisoning it. The new life of the Spirit in those who believe is a new wine that bubbles and ferments until it breaks out of the old wineskins. It could be argued that this provisionality is a vital ingredient in any doctrine of the church and of the sacraments. Living in 'the inbetween time', between the ascension and the coming of Christ in glory, the church carries its glorious treasures in earthenware vessels. The sovereign love of God may provide a means of grace, but we limit that grace if we assume it will always be delivered in the same way.

In the seventeenth century there was a debate about whether those who had been baptized as believers and those who had been baptized as infants could share fellowship in a single local church. John Bunyan was not prepared to see baptism as the sole means of entry into the church and argued for fellowship between those of differing sacramental views. Writing about these 'figurative ordinances' that are 'representations of the death and resurrection of Christ', he said:

> I count them not fundamentals of our Christianity, nor grounds or rule
> to communion with saints; servants they are, and our mystical ministers,
> to teach and instruct us in the most weighty matters of the Kingdom of
> God.[23]

While there were many contrary voices, this strand is one that continued in the years that followed. When the Oxford Baptist Church (originally founded in 1653) was reconstituted in 1780, the covenant acknowledged the presence both of those who believed Christian baptism to be the immersion of believers and of those who believed it to be the sprinkling of infants, and declared,

> Yet notwithstanding this difference of sentiment, we promise and agree
> to receive one another into the same affection and love; and for this,
> among other many reasons: because we can find no warrant in the Word
> of God to make such difference of sentiment any bar to communion at
> the Lord's Table in particular, or to church fellowship in general; and
> because the Lord Jesus receiving and owning them on both sides of the
> question, we think we ought to do so too.[24]

This is no isolated instance among Baptist churches. It demonstrates a key ecumenical principle: the recognition of other Christians as fellow believers relativizes the claims we might otherwise make about our own rites and regulations. The logic is the same as that in the story of Cornelius: a recognition of the activity of the Spirit leads to a revision of assumptions about the boundaries of the church, and God's freedom is demonstrated.

A different boundary was revised in the 1678 Orthodox Creed of the General Baptists that condemned 'the popish doctrine . . . that those infants that die without baptism or have it not actually, or in desire, are not nor cannot be saved'.[25] It denied that such infants go to purgatory or limbo and held that children dying before they are capable of choosing either good or evil—whether they are born of believing of unbelieving parents—shall be saved by the grace of God, the merit of Christ, and the work of the Holy Spirit, and thus made members of the invisible church to enjoy everlasting life. It concluded that baptism is not relevant to the issue. This time a doctrine of God's love, justice, and compassion is put before a rigid theology of baptism. It must be remembered that in the second half of the seventeenth century such views as these were viewed with political suspicion. They threatened the comprehensive infant baptismal policy of the state church, which served the need for social cohesion in a volatile, post-revolutionary society.

A constant theme is that God is not restricted by the sacraments as the only means whereby He may graciously work in the lives of men and women. Any theology that is developed concerning baptism as a means of grace must make room for this inconvenient, yet gloriously inspired, belief in the freedom of God.

3. A sacramental theology of believers' baptism

Given the wide variety of interpretations amongst Baptists, it can be argued that the word 'sacrament' may be used without threatening the concerns already explored. However, it would be wise to qualify its use. While not wanting an abstract definition that might rob baptism of its rich potential meaning, I propose that the term 'sacrament' suggests the power of symbols to link us to the depths of reality, and points us to the use by God of material means to mediate His saving action.

While not saying enough for some, this statement at least uses the word in a way that is recognizable to many Christians. The pattern offered will enable us to qualify the meaning of 'symbolism', so that we can sharpen and widen our affirmation about baptism as a means of grace.

There are a number of observations to be made before offering pointers towards a sacramental theology of believers' baptism. First, recent ecumenical studies of baptism have tended to emphasize the whole *process* of initiation, indicating that baptism is a focus of a larger process. The gift of the Spirit is seen as being at work in the reception of a child into the family of God, the nurture of a young faith, the confessing of faith, the commissioning in confirmation, and the ongoing discipleship and incorporation into the body of Christ. The importance of this cannot be overemphasized, for it removes some of the historical pressure to identify the moment and the precise means of the divine activity. This tendency encourages a perception of baptism as a part of the process of initiation for the believer and also as a part of the ongoing life of the people of God. Baptism is not an isolated event but a focus of what is continually taking place. In addition, it is recognized that it is not only initiation, but salvation itself that may be seen as a process. This widens expectations as to when and how the Holy Spirit will work in the life of the individual or indeed in the redemption of the world.

Second, seeing baptism as a part of a process enables us to broaden our understanding of how baptism may operate as a sign. While it may be only a part of the whole, it should never be referred to as 'only a sign' since it provides a lens through which the Spirit's activity may be viewed in the world and in the ongoing life of the church.[26] Our understanding of the freedom of God is clarified when His activity in baptism is seen as a pointer to His activity elsewhere, as well as an example of that wide-ranging saving activity.

Third, many interpreters have become entangled in debates about whether the word of God in baptism is objective or subjective. Yet it is evident that even subjective experiences in the life of the believer have objective causes and consequences. The very symbolism links the experience of the believer and the church with that which it signifies, so that a subjective interpretation is an important part of any explanation of baptism. Unless water is given a magical value, part of the means of grace is the subjective reinforcement offered by the symbols of water, immersion, and rising again. This strengthens the case for retaining the word 'sacrament' as it is suggestive of the link between the material, outward action and spiritual interpretations of it. Indeed, the baptism of believers increases the sacramentality of baptism by subjectively involving the one being baptized in what is happening and by offering the action of immersion. Here is a challenge to Baptists to rejoice in the sacramental nature of believers' baptism and to Paedo-Baptists to acknowledge that there is a 'sacramental loss' when the one being baptized is not aware of what is happening and when the action is affusion not immersion.[27] There is a similar objective/subjective richness for the congregation that shares in the event, and this widens the reference to include the church, as well as the believer, in what is happening.

(i) A sacrament of proclamation

Baptism is a proclamation of the gospel of Jesus Christ. It links the person being baptized with the example of Jesus at his baptism, with the command of the risen Christ, and with the Christian experience of salvation. As a demonstration of forgiveness of sins, a representation of the death, burial, and resurrection of Jesus, an expression of the believer's union with the risen Lord, and a celebration of incorporation into the body of Christ, baptism proclaims and enacts.

Baptists have long emphasized the eloquent witness that a baptismal service offers to others. It challenges those who have not responded to Christ to consider the demands of discipleship and encourages those who have been long in the faith to remember their own baptism for encouragement and challenge. Yet the proclamation must be more than simply someone confessing his or her faith; otherwise we could dispense with the water! Proclamation is to be found in the whole fabric of meanings, only some of which will be unravelled in the course of a lifetime. Here is the proclamation of a mystery. The mystery of Christ and our salvation demands a sign greater than words; it requires a proclamation that goes beyond definitions and easy statements. The Word has become—and continues to become—flesh, and Christians continue to see his glory. Here is no easily packaged evangelism but the presentation of the gospel in the profound symbol of baptism.

This focus on Jesus is important. The Incarnation provides the clue whereby God is identified at work around us. The stories of the baptism of Jesus and the institution of the Last Supper provide a narrative framework (Augustine's *verbum*) for the sacraments. Just as in the Lord's Supper the bringing to mind includes the cross, resurrection, and ascension of Jesus Christ, so in baptism that which begins at the river Jordan passes through Galilee, Golgotha, and Emmaus.

Union with Jesus Christ is more than the following of an example; it becomes the proclamation of the gospel of Christ. It is meaningless to divide what God does from what the believer or the church does, for in this proclamation the Holy Spirit is working—in those who act and those who witness, in those who speak and those who hear. At the centre of it all, the Word of God made flesh is enfleshed again in the fellowship of His people and the testimony of a new disciple.

(ii) A sacrament of partnership

Baptism may be seen as a focus of the divine-human encounter. Despite the variety of sacramental theologies, there is a measure of agreement in affirming the work of the Spirit and the importance of a human response. Disagreement sets in when we try to locate the divine activity and identify the agents in the human response. For example, Baptists would argue that the response is firstly on the part of the person being baptized and then also by the fellowship of the church. Paedo-Baptists would see the response in the actions and promises of the sponsors, though finally only the faith of the church is required—and that might even be found in the single figure of the administrator.[28] In locating the role of divine grace, we must first recognize that the saving acts of the gospel in the birth, life, death, and resurrection of Jesus Christ are the foundational mode of divine activity. While Christians might disagree about whose faith is important, Christians must acknowledge that faith itself is a gift and the human response is a part of the divine action.

The more we see baptism as the focus of a redemptive process, the less important become the questions of where and how God is at work. What we *can* affirm is that baptism is a sacrament of partnership where God enters into partnership with the church and the person being baptized. The individual and the church also enter into partnership; and for those Baptists who refuse to separate baptism and church membership, this is demonstrated in an eloquent way, not only through the celebration and the prayers of those gathered for worship, but by the commissioning for service through the laying on of hands and by the reception into membership with the right hand of fellowship.

In his exploration of the doctrine of the Incarnation, D. M. Baillie used what he called the 'central paradox of grace' as a means of approaching the paradox of the true God and the true humanity in Christ. He saw in the interaction of the Holy Spirit with any human personality a model that illuminated what the church seeks to affirm in a unique way about the Incarnation.[29] In one sense, that linkage is reversed in baptism; the doctrine of the Incarnation reminds us of the embodied way in which the Spirit seeks to work. Indeed, we could argue that the Incarnation continues in the life of discipleship as the Spirit beckons, stirs, cleanses, and inspires the faltering steps of one who would follow Christ. Between the Incarnation and the life of faith lie the waters of baptism where the believer abandons the past and seeks a new life of partnership not only with other Christians but in union with Christ.

Partnership should not be undervalued as a theological category, since it points not only to the paradox of grace but to the profound mystery of collaboration within the Trinity and the trinitarian basis for fellowship, worship, and obedient faith.

(iii) A sacrament of presence

Any use of the word sacrament must have as its foundation the doctrine of the Incarnation, where creation and redemption are united in God's saving action. The symbolic aspect of baptism must therefore not be ignored, with its many layers of possible meaning. The *mysterion* of God's salvation is offered in an embodied form that defies simple, verbal explanation.[30] While the symbolism will be controlled by Scripture, the tightness of control will differ with different traditions.

The relationship between baptism and the Incarnation is clear in a number of different ways. Baptism uses water, a physical substance, part of creation. Water thus represents the physical world that is not only a part of the biblical vision for the final consummation, but an indication that God may come to us outside the church, mediated through substances and situations that make up His world. A recognition of God inthe sacramental act of baptizing opens our eyes to the sacramental nature of reality. An affirmation of God's presence in the sacraments of the church only has meaning insofar as it points to His sacramental presence in the world Christ died to save.

The Incarnation enables us to see the Word made flesh in each baby and each crucifixion and opens our eyes to the divine glory in unexpected places. The sacraments become a celebration of creation and a statement of hope that God will redeem His world.

The Incarnation gives meaning to baptism, for the believer is baptized into union with Christ Jesus. Here is an act of obedient love to the command of Christ and a recognition that just as God's action became enfleshed in Jesus, so it must continue to be enfleshed in the historical reality of His people. In baptism the believer is united with the one who has entered into solidarity with sinful humanity that all the world might cry 'glory'.

(iv) A sacrament of prophecy

We must not ignore the distinction between calling baptism a *sign* and calling it a *symbol*. We have seen that as a symbol it offers a point of reflection and communion, the promise of depths to be plumbed. As a sign it points beyond the here and now in warning and promises, for the whole fate of Jesus is telescoped into Christian baptism. When we enter the waters at his baptism, we are buried and raised with him. Union with Christ promises a cross as well as a crown. Jesus asked James and John if they could be baptized with the baptism he was to undergo, and this reference to his death is one that is always present in Christian baptism.[31] Here is a sign that the Christian enters the path of life that will pass through the world that crucified Jesus. The contradiction of the cross is a fundamental feature of Christian living, and baptism offers not only the clue but the means to cope with such a prospect.

As the sacrament of incorporation into the body of Christ and the means of entry into his church, baptism links the fate of the believer to the mission and witness of the people of God. The church is called to be a sign of the Kingdom of God in a world that sees the cross as foolishness and weakness. The sacraments are offered to the church as a means of enabling the church to be a sacrament of the Kingdom. In baptism a counterculture begins with an act of repentance, a turning from evil and a burying of the old values and priorities. The prophetic witness of the church is not primarily the press release or even the political analysis, but the baptism and the martyrdom of the saints of God.

(v) A sacrament of promise

Baptism points forward as a sign to the life of discipleship and beyond the struggle to the final consummation of all things. The gift of the Spirit in baptism cannot be separated from the prophecy of Joel and the Pentecostal experience of the church. The Holy Spirit is far more than an indwelling presence or even an inspirer and enabler of discipleship and communion. The Spirit is the pledge of what is in store for us, the seal of God's promises, the inspirer of a hope that rocks us out of a complacent acceptance of the way things are.[32]

The sacrament of baptism ought not to be seen as a delivery mechanism of assurance and certainty, but the sign and seal of God's covenant promises. The baptism of believers gains a new dimension when faith is not seen so much as an assent to a creed as a commitment to living a life of faith. The recognition of the freedom of God returns as a gadfly to worry and disturb any automatic assumptions of grace bestowed through rightly ordered ritual. What is offered in baptism is not certainty of salvation, but union with one whose promises can be trusted.

4. Baptism and the sacramental freedom of God

Such an emphasis on the sovereign freedom of God enables us both to declare a rich and exciting series of affirmations about baptism while at the same time avoiding some of the historic dangers of sacramental theology. To say, 'God is here' is good. To say, 'God is here but not only here' is better. To say, 'God is here, therefore we can meet Him here and be equipped to meet Him elsewhere' is best of all.

The freedom of God means that He is free to work through the means of grace that He has given to His church. But this freedom also declares that He need not only work through such means. It is important to recognize that the Holy Spirit operates beyond as well as within the church, because that very truth liberates us to expect the Spirit within the worship of the people of God. Because we are freed from the fears of mechanical sacramentalism, we are freed to approach baptism as an opportunity for celebration and fruitfulness where the Spirit moves powerfully amongst a praising and responsive people.

We must never forget that there are, from a human perspective, limits to divine freedom. Those limits are most clearly seen in the revelation of the divine nature in Jesus Christ. The Spirit is the spirit of Jesus, and God's freedom is limited in the sense that He will not act contrary to what He has shown us in Jesus. Again, baptism becomes a focus of divine activity but not its entirety: the act is Christocentric, and its fulness is in its centre—not its boundary. God is faithful, and all that we might expect is transformed in the one with whom we are buried and raised.

God's freedom refuses to allow grace to be dispensed on demand or as the result of correctly followed procedures. However, that freedom is the freedom of the God who freely gave His son for our salvation, the freedom of the one who laid out his hands to be pinned to a cross, the freedom of one who lay bound in a borrowed tomb. Here is no capricious deity refusing to be held accountable or truculently ignoring the plea for justice. Here is the freedom of one who freely loves and freely forgives and who promises to meet us both in the waters of baptism and in the world to which we are sent.

Notes to Chapter 2

[1]There is an important distinction between adult baptism and the baptism of believers. It is the latter that is practised by Baptists with no rigid assumptions about the age of the person being baptized.

[2]The meaning of the word 'ordinance' is something that is recorded in the New Testament as having been commanded, or ordained, by Jesus to the disciples and, by extension, the church. While other practices have been referred to by the word ordinance (e.g. footwashing: 'I have set you an example'. John 13:15), the word has normally referred to the two so-called 'Gospel sacraments' of baptism and the Lord's Supper. For ordinance described as a sign, see Article XXIX of the Particular Baptist *Second London Confession* (1677), in W. L. Lumpkin, *Baptist Confessions of Faith* (Judson Press, Philadelphia, 1959), pp. 290-91.

[3]In 1612, Thomas Helwys published *A Short Declaration of the Mystery of Iniquity* and personally dedicated a copy to King James I; he stated, 'Let them

be heretikes, Turcks, Jewes, or whatsoever, it apperteynes not to the earthly power to punish them in the least measure' (p. 69).

[4]For an account of the development of sacramental theology, see D. Forrester, J. I. H. McDonald, and G. Tellini, *Encounter with God*, (T. & T. Clark, Edinburgh, 1983), pp. 57ff.

[5]A comprehensive study would include a systematic exposition of New Testament material with regard to baptism. N. Clark makes this point in *An Approach to the Theology of the Sacraments* (SCM, London, 1956), p. 71. However, the themes of sacramental theology offer signposts towards areas that need exploring. Here this exploration takes place within a discussion of historical theology, but a thorough treatment would need to interact more fully with the Bible.

[6]Augustine distinguished between the *signum*, or visible material element such as water, and the *virtus sacramenti*, or inward grace conveyed by the sacrament. He also claimed that the *verbum*, or spoken formula pronounced by the minister, linked the two: 'Take away the Word and the water is nothing but water.' (*On the Gospel of John* 80:3)

[7]In a series of sermons preached in 1849–1850 that were published by E. B. Pusey in 1869 as *Village Sermons on the Baptismal Service*.

[8]J. M. Cramp, *Baptist History from the Foundation of the Christian Church to the Present Time* (Elliot Stock, London, 1871), p. 16.

[9]However, see Martin Reardon, *Christian Initiation—A Policy for the Church of England* (Church House, London, 1991), p. 14: 'This teaching is sometimes said to imply that there is an objective gift of something called grace, which, however, lies totally dormant in the soul unless awakened by God's gift of faith. Such an interpretation of *ex opere operato* sees it as an aspect of the "reification" of grace (making grace a thing rather than a relationship) about which many modern theologians, including Roman Catholic ones, complain. . . . in its pure and original form, [*ex opere operato*] asserts that baptism is a gift and work of God that is not nullified by the unworthiness of the minister who administers it. It does not deny that faith is necessary in the recipient if it is to be really effectual. God has offered and made his gift in baptism. To be effective the gift has also to be received. Where it is not received in faith, it is not efficacious.' In a discussion paper about baptismal policy in the church of England, Reardon is concerned to make this explanation about the *ex opere operato* doctrine so that it cannot be used as a justification of 'indiscriminate' infant baptism.

[10]E.g. Rom 8:14-30.

[11]The question of development in doctrine and practice is not an easy one to resolve. Even when we have recognized the contextual nature of the biblical material and the contextual needs of the developing and contemporary church, we are faced with the tension of continuity and discontinuity. Infant baptism is a sharp challenge to Baptists, not only because of the overwhelming testimony

of most of the Christian church that the Spirit has led them in this direction, but because of the claim that those truths proclaimed in infant baptism are biblical truths (Note 5 above). This issue is not only about theological method, but about the ongoing interaction of the Word of God with the People of God.

[12]Lumpkin, op. cit., p. 167 (Article XL).

[13]Pastoral advice for special circumstances is given in the Baptist Union of Great Britain publication *Patterns and Prayers for Christian Worship* (Oxford University Press and BUGB, Oxford, 1991), p. 97.

[14]Baptists are sometimes accused of advocating 'salvation by works' as it is claimed that the emphasis on the faith of the believer points more to the human response than to the divine initiative. However, properly understood, faith should be seen not so much as doctrinal assent as faith in and reliance upon God.

[15]E.g. C. H. Spurgeon, 'Baptismal Regeneration' in *Metropolitan Tabernacle Pulpit*, Vol X, 1864 (Passmore & Alabaster, London, 1865), no. 573.

[16]Horton Davies, *Worship and Theology in England from Cranmer to Hooker 1534–1603* (Princeton University Press, New York, 1970) p. 342.

[17]This is a summary of Smyth's views as abstracted from his *The Differences of the Churches of the Separation* in *A Dissuasive from the Errours of the Time* (1645) by Robert Baillie, p. 29, quoted in Horton Davies, op.cit., p. 342.

[18]Helwys, in a letter of September 26, 1608, explains that 'we suppose it will prove the truth that all books even the originals themselves must be laid aside in the time of spiritual worship, yet still retaining the reading and interpreting of the Scriptures in the church for the preparing to worship, judging doctrine, deciding of controversies as the ground of our faith and of our whole profession,'; cited Champlin Burrage, *The Early English Dissenters in the Light of Recent Research* II (Cambridge University Press, Cambridge, 1912), p. 167.

[19]Many Baptist writes have spent considerable time in expounding the meaning of *baptizo* in the New Testament, for example, R. Ingham, *A Handbook of Christian Baptism* (Simpkin & Marshall, London, 1865); *Baptism, Its Subjects* (Stock, London, 1871); A. Carson, *Baptism in Its Mode and* Subjects (Houlston & Stoneman, London, 1844).

[20]E.g. R. C. Walton, *The Gathered Community* (Carey Press, London, 1946); A. Gilmore (Ed.), *Christian Baptism* (Lutterworth, London, 1959); Gilmore (Ed.) *The Pattern of the Church: A Baptist View* (Lutterworth, London, 1963); G. R. Beasley-Murray, *Baptism in the New Testament* (Macmillan, London, 1962); Beasley-Murray, *Baptism Today and Tomorrow* (Macmillan, London, 1966).

[21]Quoted in E. A. Payne, *The Fellowship of Believers,* 2nd edition (Carey Kingsgate Press, London, 1952), p. 88.

[22]Acts 10:44ff and 8:17 respectively.

[23]*Works of Bunyan*, (Ed. George Offor), Vol. II, (Blackie, Glasgow, 1855), p. 604; quoted in Payne, op. cit., pp. 63f.

[24]E. C. Alden, *The Old Church at New Road. A Contribution to the History of Oxford Nonconformity* (Alden, Oxford, 1904), pp. 14-15.

[25]Lumpkin, op. cit., p. 318 (Article XXVIII)

[26]Paul Tillich makes a similar point but by making a distinction between symbol and sign: 'The symbol participates in the reality which is symbolized. Therefore, one should never say "only a symbol".' *Systematic Theology*, Vol.2 (University of Chicago Press, Chicago, 1957), p. 10.

[27]While washing is an image present in the action of affusion, both washing and union with Christ in his death and resurrection are evident in the action of immersion.

[28]See the debate in Reardon, op.cit., concerning the faith of the parents and sponsors. He asks, 'If the godparents are representing the church, should not at least one of them represent the local Christian community where the infant is to be baptized, and where he or she is likely to live at least for the foreseeable future?' (p. 25), though others' views about those who need to exercise faith are to be found in the additional papers added to the document.

[29]D. M. Baillie, *God Was in Christ: An Essay in Incarnation and Atonement* (Faber & Faber, London, 1948), especially pp.114-132.

[30]For the relationship between the biblical *mysterion* and the Latin *sacramentum*, see Forrester, McDonald, Tellini, op. cit., pp. 57ff.

[31]This is the theological basis for the early church's recognition of the 'baptism of martyrdom' where believers were martyred before they could be baptized.

[32]1 Cor 1:22; 5:5; Eph 1:14.

3
Baptism and Creation

PAUL S. FIDDES

Lovers lie around in it.
Broken glass is found in it
Grass
I like that stuff . . .

Elephants get sprayed with it
Scotch is made with it
Water
I like that stuff

Clergy are dumbfounded by it
Bones are surrounded by it
Flesh
I like that stuff . . .

Well I like that stuff
Yes I like that stuff
The earth
Is made of earth
And I like that stuff

So a modern poet, Adrian Mitchell, celebrates the materials of the natural world.[1] In some instances he may be right that 'clergy are dumbfounded by it', but we should also recall C. S. Lewis' happy phrase that 'God likes matter; after all, he made it.' Indeed, within the Christian tradition the sacraments are pieces of matter that God takes and uses as special places of encounter with Himself; grace transforms nature, and grace is nothing less than God's gracious coming to us and to His world. The personal, triune God who is always present to influence and change human personalities makes Himself present in a deeper way through water, bread, and wine. In the sacraments God's action in creation and redemption thus fuses into a particular focus.

Now, with regard to baptism, those in other Christian traditions might suppose that among Baptists there would be the richest expression of the link between redemption and creation. Total immersion, and the involvement of persons who have conscious faith, means that there is the greater opportunity for sacred drama involving substantial contact with the element of water. There is potential for a multimedia drama that will involve the person and the community at every level. As a matter of fact, however, Baptists have to confess that there has been a flight from the 'stuff' of creation. There has been, let it be admitted, a concealing of baptisteries under the floor, an underplaying of the use of the water and the emphasizing of the 'testimony' part, a lack of a sense of drama, and (though this is fortunately fast passing) an insulation of the minister from the water by the use of incongruous waders.

Despite this tendency, I want to affirm that the Baptist practice of believers' baptism does make possible a recovery of the sense of the baptismal water as an actual element of the natural world, as well as a metaphor of God's redemptive activity. This location of baptism in creation also relates, I want to show, to wider issues of Baptist self-identity and to the Baptist contribution to the ecumenical scene.

The symbol of water touches human experience at many points; descent into water, sprinkling with water, and passing through water have been part not only of religious rituals but key images in the written and visual arts. We may here conveniently identify five motifs connected with water that have been important for the Judaeo-Christian tradition: birth, cleansing, conflict, refreshment, and journey. These, I believe, all have a foundation in natural life and thus arouse deep-laid associations in the unconscious as well as lay hold of our conscious memories. In his book *Christianity and Symbolism*, F. W. Dillistone maintains that 'to find a way of allowing baptism to exercise its power within the Christian community at the deepest level of the human psyche is one of the most urgent tasks of our day', and he finds the urgency to stem from the fact that these natural images are so powerful that if they are not sanctified within a Christian context 'they will almost certainly present themselves in demonic forms'.[2] This present chapter is an attempt to suggest ways to meet the challenge of a scholar who was my former teacher, and I am glad to acknowledge that my review of the motifs connected with water owes not a little to Dillistone's own pioneering discussion.

In addition, however, to the natural context of these primordial images of water, they have been central images as the people of God have reflected upon their past experience in history, and as they have formed convictions about the way that God acted redemptively for them in that public arena. Thus the symbols are rich in reference to both creation and redemption, and in particular they have been grounded in history through the life, death, and resurrection of Jesus. The power of the baptismal event lies in its drawing upon experiences of both nature and history, and its uniting of them in worship.

1. Birth

In the first place, the descent into water within a religious ceremony has often been associated with a return to the womb, and so with regeneration and the renewal of life. There is an immediate reference here to the fact that the unborn foetus lives in water within the womb and perhaps a more distant recollection of the ancient concept that the waters of the underworld were the place whence life issued. The latter picture is no doubt connected with the former, especially where rivers are portrayed in ancient texts as issuing from the 'womb' or the 'vagina' of the earth.[3] Conversely then, the vagina of a woman was often described poetically as a 'well' or 'fountain' of life (cf. Prov 5:15). Woven into the whole complex of imagery is also the breaking of the waters in the process of birth; the child is nurtured in the life-giving waters and is then born 'through water'. It is hardly surprising in the light of all this that Carl Jung interpreted mythical expressions of descent into water as a descent into the womb of the unconscious mind, which must be penetrated before new life and creativity can be born.[4] We may trace then, in the human psyche, a deeply embedded urge to return to the waters whence we have come and from there to make a new beginning.

The direct connection of water with birth and regeneration is actually rather rare in the Old Testament. Perhaps Genesis 1:2 presents the Spirit of God 'brooding' over the waters of chaos, bringing creation to birth as if from a cosmic womb (cf. Job 38:8—'the sea . . . burst in flood from the womb'). Birth imagery is more often used as a way of expressing redemptive experience in history, as Israel is addressed in prophetic oracle as having been a child born and brought to adulthood through such experiences as slavery in Egypt, exodus, and wilderness wandering.[5] In His purpose to bring about a new exodus for His people, Yahweh is also described as being like a woman in the pains of childbirth.[6] Nevertheless, any association of passing through the waters of the Red Sea with images of birth is left implicit, while (as we shall see shortly) images of conflict are highly explicit.

The historicizing of birth imagery, however, comes to a remarkable fusion with the water of baptism in the gospel accounts of the baptism of Jesus in the Jordan River when he is greeted by the heavenly voice with the words, 'You are my Son' (Matt 3:17, Mark 1:11, Luke 3:22). To make clear the reminiscence of Psalm 2:7, other ancient versions of Luke's account add, 'Today I have begotten you.' This psalm appears to contain a liturgy in which kings of ancient Israel would be greeted by Yahweh as having been adopted as His sons, and so 'brought to birth' in their coronation.[7] This affirmation is now applied in a special way to Jesus in his baptism, and the image of birth is underlined by Mark and Matthew since they describe the announcement as happening at the very moment when Jesus 'came up out' of the water. There is, of course, no implication here that Jesus himself is in need of spiritual rebirth (as Matthew makes clear in his account, 3:14-15); rather, he completely identifies himself with an Israel that is in need of regeneration, and fully embodies in himself the sonship by which the Israelite kings had failed to live, despite all the hopes expressed for them.

The Fourth Gospel carries on the association of water with birth, probably relating this to baptism in the expression 'born of water and the Spirit' (John 3:5). Already, it has been argued, the primary meaning of Jewish baptism of Gentile proselytes had become that of rebirth.[8] Early Christian theologians certainly have no hesitation in comparing the baptismal pool to a womb; Cyril of Jerusalem affirms, 'this wholesome water has become for you both a tomb and a mother',[9] and Ephraem the Syrian exclaims:

> O womb which daily brings forth without pain the sons of the kingdom of heaven! They descend indeed with their faults and their stains, but they rise up pure as infants. For Baptism becomes a second womb for them.[10]

The natural association between baptism and birth has, in fact, been most strongly felt in recent times by women Christian ministers in administering baptism. I heard one woman, for example, speaking movingly of her experience of baptizing her own son as being 'like giving birth to him for a second time.' In the dramatic setting of believers' baptism, as she raised him from the waters that had enclosed him, the words of Nicodemus about the paradox of rebirth took on a special poignance: 'Can a man enter his mother's womb a second time and be born?'

2. Cleansing

The second major motif to which I draw attention is that of water as a symbol of spiritual cleansing. The sense of a need to be purified at every level of our being is another deeply embedded human feeling; the universal use of water for washing the body provides an image for the 'washing out' of inner taint in the mind and spirit. We notice that after a particularly unpleasant experience a person may say, 'I had to take a bath because I felt unclean all over', and we understand Lady Macbeth's anguish after the bloody murder of Duncan when she complains that 'all the perfumes of Arabia will not sweeten this little hand.'

We find the use of water rituals for purification in every known religion. The Old Testament legal codes have many instructions for purificatory rites, as did the community at Qumran with its multiple baths. The bathings and washing of clothes prescribed in the book of Leviticus are intended to prepare the priests and the people for encounter with the holy presence of God, and such rituals stress the integration of the spiritual and physical dimensions of life in the understanding of ancient Israel. Positively, they bear witness to the psychosomatic wholeness of the human being and raise echoes in the modern concern for 'holism' and creation-centred spirituality; negatively, they could lead to what we might diagnose as a confusion between physical and spiritual uncleanness, as for example in the instructions for ritual washing following contact with the dead and lepers and for the so-called 'purification' of women following childbirth. Such an anxiety about purification could lead to the exclusion of people as 'unclean' and to the kind of mechanical rituals of washing of hands and vessels that Jesus later condemns (Mark 7:1-8). On the whole, however, the Old Testament affirms quite impressively that outward cleansing without a 'clean heart' would not fit people for the experience of the holy:

> Purge me with hyssop, and I shall be clean;
> wash me, and I shall be whiter then snow. . . .
> Create in me a clean heart, O God,

and put a new and right spirit within me. . . .
The sacrifice acceptable to God is a broken spirit,
a broken and contrite heart, O God, you will not despise.
                                        (Ps 51:7, 10, 17)

This psalm, with its mention of sacrifices and 'burnt offerings' (vv. 16-17), reminds us that alongside the rites of purifying through water there was also the purifying through blood in the 'sin-offering' (*hattat*). Here the rituals of cleansing begin to interact with the concerns of 'atonement', that is, the 'making at-one' of a holy God and sinful human beings. It seems quite clear that the purpose of the sin-offering was not to propitiate God but to expiate sins, that is to 'wash them away' through the cleansing power of blood;[11] the sacrifice both expiated the sin and purified the sinner.[12] At Qumran, when it was no longer possible to make the atoning sacrifice, they quite naturally understood sacrifice to be replaced by rituals of washing and bathing, while at the same time they fully recognized the limitations of an outward ceremony. As the Rule of the community puts it, 'a man . . . shall not be cleansed by all the waters of washing. . . . for as long as he scorns the ordinances of God.'[13]

Whether the cleansing agent is water or blood, the Old Testament rituals are drawing upon a deep human desire for purification. They are also affirming that God Himself must act through these natural elements to purge human lives of uncleanness. As with the symbol of birth, Israel also therefore historicized the symbol of cleansing. The prophet Ezekiel portrays Israel as having been washed clean by Yahweh in His adoption of her as a nation in past history (Ezek 16:9), and he and other prophets look forward to a new age when there will be a complete cleansing in a single once-for-all purgation (Zech 13:1, Mal 3:1ff, Ezek 36:25).

All these strands are taken up into the New Testament. For the Fourth Gospel, Israel's hopes for a final 'washing' of human life have been fulfilled in history in the ministry of Jesus (John 9:7; 13:5). Atonement has also been located in one decisive historic moment, and purification is a primary image by means of which New Testament writers understand the experience of reconciliation and forgiveness they have received through the cross of Jesus. They interpret his death as a once-for-all expiating sacrifice and a purification achieved through the sprinkling of blood. It is true that the image of 'washing' from sin is only applied a few times explicitly to baptism,[14] but this ritual symbolizes and actualizes an atonement that is all about cleansing and for which the New Testament writer uses the same complex interaction between the agency of water and blood that we find in more ancient texts. For instance, in Hebrews 10:20-22 the ancient 'Day of Atonement' rites of both sprinkling with blood and washing with water are applied to the effects of the death of Christ, together with an unmistakeable reference to baptism through which these benefits are received. Believers are urged to approach God 'with our hearts sprinkled clean from an evil conscience and our bodies washed with pure water'.

As a footnote from recent times, I was personally present at a meeting of the Baptist World Alliance in Seoul in 1990, when the South Korean Minister of Culture, a Buddhist, greeted the congress members with a speech constructed entirely around the association of baptism with purification. Noting that there was to be an open-air service of baptism in the River Han that flows through the middle of Seoul, he expressed the hope that this act would be the beginning of the spiritual cleansing of the whole city and society, and that this would lead to a purification of the waters of the river itself from the industrial pollution that was spoiling it. Thus in the context of modern environmental problems, the image of cleansing retains its archetypal power.

3. Conflict

Third, the symbol of water evokes a sense of conflict and the overcoming of hostile powers. Faced with the tremendous force of a tidal wave, or irresistible floods, or the continuous threat of drowning in storms at sea, it is natural that water should also appear as an enemy in the human consciousness. Early myths in the Ancient Near East conceive of the act of creation as a victory over the chaos monster who either is, or dwells in, the Sea. So also in the biblical account, creation cuts a place for human beings to live between the seas; the creator God holds back the unruly disorder of the waters and liberates the land (Job 26:12-13; 38:8-11; cf. Gen 1:6-10).

In ancient Israel this theme of conflict and victory in creation rarely, however, stands on its own but is connected to the redemptive acts of God in Israel's life and history. In Psalm 74 the writer recalls God's choice of Israel as His people and Mount Zion as His dwelling place, and among these 'saving acts' He counts the 'cleaving of the sea monster in two' and the regular coming of summer and winter since then. Similarly, in Psalm 89:9-10 the overcoming of the watery chaos monster and the elevating of David to kingship merge into one focus. Most notably, Isaiah of Babylon fuses the imagery of the dividing and curbing of the chaotic sea at creation with the dividing of the waters of the Red Sea at the Exodus, and so promises a new Exodus for the people in exile (Isa 43:16-19; 51:9-11); God will once again 'make the ocean depths a path for the redeemed.'

So, in the overcoming of the waters of death and disaster, creation and redemption merge into one flowing process. In the rainbow sign the priestly theologians found assurance that God was continuing to hold back the waters of chaos that had broken over the earth in the great flood (Gen 9:12-17). The Psalms also speak of a continual redemption from death in the life of the individual; when in illness God holds back the forces of death and restores health, then He is liberating from the power of the underworld (Sheol), a threat that is depicted as taking a grip on the sufferer's throat, as the monster of chaos, stifling him with the weight of a great flood of water (Ps 18:16).

The association of water with a hostile power, and ultimately with death itself, is the predominant meaning that baptism carries in the New Testament. Jesus in his baptism in the waters of Jordan prefigures his plunging into the waters of death at the cross and (at least in later patristic thought) his descent into the waters of Hades. Looking to his death, he enquires of his disciples, 'Can you be baptized with the baptism with which I am baptized?' (Mark 10:38) As the Apostle Paul explains, in passing through these waters Christ overcomes the principalities and powers that hold human life in bondage, unmasking and exposing them for the idols and the tyrants that they are, and showing that they have no authority over him by rising from death. Paul urges that we are identified with Christ in baptism; we share in the passage of Christ through the deep waters of death as we pass through the waters of baptism, and so we also share in his victory over the dark powers (Col 2:12-15; Rom 6:1-5). Christ participates in the most bitter depths of human death in order that we might participate in his resurrection. In 1 Peter 3:18-22 this idea is similarly presented, while the writer also finds an apt analogy between baptism and Noah's ark that provided survival in the onslaught of the Great Flood.

In the Baptist tradition, total immersion has always been valued as a vivid portrayal of death and resurrection—a descent into the 'grave' and a being raised with Christ. However, this has too often been interpreted in a merely individualistic fashion as a personal dying to self, and the wider symbolism of a confrontation with the hostile powers has been lost. The powers that hold human beings in oppression must also be understood in terms of political and economic structures and governing authorities, and thus as Brian Haymes argues in another paper in this volume, baptism is a 'political act.'

4. Journey

Connected with this image of water as a hostile power to be overcome is the fourth motif of a journey over water. Both involve 'passing through the water' and involve danger. But the journey image is less about the hazards on the way than the leaving behind of one territory or area of life and the setting out for another. The water is a kind of boundary situation. Since rivers and seas form natural barriers to human travel and conquest, as well as natural markers for the ownership of land, it is hardly surprising that the motif of 'crossing the water' has so rooted a place in human consciousness. In Neo-Platonist imagery the soul at the beginning of life makes its journey across the waters of generation riding a dolphin, or it is depicted like a seashell cast up from the waves onto the shore. In fact, through various transformations in the history of Christian art, the seashell frequently makes its appearance today in ceremonies of infant baptism as a scoop for the water. At the other end of life, the last frontier of the river of death appears in the ancient world as the Styx and in Christian art as the Jordan, as for example in the final triumphant chapter of John Bunyan's *Pilgrim's Progress*.

Ancient Israel typically understood its experience in more historic terms and saw its 'crossing the water' as leaving behind one style of life and entering a new covenant relationship. In crossing the Red Sea they separated from life in Egypt as slaves, and in crossing the River Jordan they separated from the nomadic life of the desert (Josh 1). Passage through water was a mark of separation for the whole nation, as circumcision was a mark of separation from the other nations for the individual Israelite.

In viewing baptism as a replacement for the rite of circumcision, the New Testament understands baptism to be similarly a mark of separation from past life and the kingdom of darkness and a passing into new kingdom territory. Baptism is a moment of complete reevaluation of what really matters in life. With its associations of 'crossing the water', baptism actually fits better than circumcision into the network of concepts concerning leaving and entering phases of life. In fact, it is even possible that the development of Jewish proselyte baptism had already been prompted by the story of deliverance at and through the Red Sea, the rite of baptism portraying even better than circumcision the separation of the Gentile from his past life and his entrance into the people of God. Paul's exegesis in 1 Corinthians 10:1-2 may, it is suggested, reflect a rabbinic justification for such proselyte baptism: 'our ancestors all passed through the Red Sea; and so they all received baptism into the fellowship of Moses in cloud and sea'.

Within the history of the Christian church, the act of receiving baptism has similarly meant a costly separation from one kind of culture and entrance into the new humanity in Christ. In parts of Africa and Asia today, the receiving of Christian baptism carries the cost of expulsion from family, tribal, and societal life. In this sense too, baptism is 'a political act'.

5. Refreshment

In the final motif water is a means and a symbol of refreshment. The sprinkling of water that cleanses from taint also produces a renewal of energies. The pouring of water, whether for drinking or for bathing, carries the sense of renewal of life. Especially in a hot country, bathing in water reinvigorates the body just as streams irrigate a dry land.

The natural basis of this symbol needs no further elaboration. However, we notice that once more the Israelite theologians and poets gave it a definitely historical location. The story of the striking of water from a rock by Moses in the desert wilderness placed the gift of water among the redemptive acts of God in history (Num 20:1-12), and the incident was often recalled.[15] As the prophets lament the exhausting of national energies, they also look forward to a renewal by Yahweh, and they identify the future pouring out of life-giving water with the Spirit of Yahweh (e.g. Isa 44:3, cf. Ezek 43:1-11).

The 'pouring out' of the Spirit is thus associated closely in the New Testament with baptism (Mark 1:10; 1 Cor 12:12-13), together with the image of 'drinking' the Spirit. The Fourth Gospel offers a fusion of these images, as it depicts an invitation that Jesus makes on the last day of the Feast of Tabernacles, when large jars of water are drawn from the fountain of Gihon and poured out on the altar; as the water is poured, Jesus invites the spiritually thirsty to drink from the 'living waters' of the Spirit that flow out of his heart (John 7:37-9). The Old Testament motif of water-from-the-rock also probably lies behind the evangelist's account (cf. 1 Cor 10:4). It is possible (though not certain), as Raymond Brown argues,[16] that the evangelist intends a reference to baptism here, as he may also intend in the earlier story of the Samaritan woman at the well and Jesus' promise there of 'the water of life' (John 4:14). Both stories and Jesus' sayings within them were frequently connected to baptism by the early church fathers, and the scene with the woman at the well appears in early catacomb art as a symbol for baptism. There is, of course, no simple equation of the 'living water' with the water of baptism; rather, drinking the living water (the Spirit) is associated with baptism since the gift of the Spirit is received through it.

6. The communication of grace

All this means that if the drama of baptism is properly arranged, the contact with the element of water should arouse a range of experiences in the person baptized and in the community that shares in the act. Immersion into water—with both its shocking and pleasurable sensations—can evoke a sense of descent into the womb, a washing away of what is unclean, an encounter with a hostile force, a passing through a boundary marker, and reinvigoration. In all these aspects, water is a place in the material world that can become a 'rendezvous'[17] with the crucified and risen Christ.

It may be protested that tracing a kaleidoscope of natural motifs as I have done leads to the bewildering impression that baptism means anything and everything, and therefore nothing in particular. However, just as the Old Testament writers appeal to the natural symbol of water to express their experience of God's acts in history, so the various aspects of the baptismal water enable us to participate in the death and resurrection of Jesus. This is the controlling event, and to it all the motifs relate, although (as I have suggested) the third motif of conflict makes the most obvious reference. Immersion into water conveys the 'shock' of dying, of being overwhelmed by alien powers; coming out from water conveys resurrection, an emergence to new life in which the hostile powers have not been left behind but in which there is new energy to deal with them.

Now, I want to stress here that the water in baptism is not merely a visual aid to help us understand various spiritual concepts: in its sheer materiality or 'stuffness' it actually communicates the presence of the transcendent God. A created thing provides places and opportunities for a transforming encounter. From an Old Testament perspective we can understand this as based in God's nature as both Creator and Redeemer, as Lord of both the cosmos and history. But we can gain a deeper appreciation of the rooting of sacrament in creation if we follow the apostle Paul's insight that through baptism we participate in the 'body' of Christ. In Jesus Christ, God has committed Himself to the utmost extent to materiality, to human flesh. But with His eternal decision that He should identify Himself totally (in act and being) with a human son, and that this son should be the means of creating a new human community, God also commits Himself to taking on the whole body of the universe. Human flesh is, after all, entangled with the entire organic structure of the cosmos; it could not exist without this context and community in which it is embedded.

Both creation and incarnation therefore tell us that the God who relates Himself to human beings also has a kind of relation, and evokes a kind of response, within created reality at every level. We hardly yet have a language to describe this reciprocation between God and His natural creation, but the Scriptures provide a poetic portrayal of it with images such as the seas roaring the praise of God, the rivers clapping their hands in joy, the cedars whirling in adoration, the skies speaking words of witness, the sea monsters playing with Yahweh, and the whole universe groaning as if in the pangs of childbirth, longing for God to set it free.[18] Thus God makes covenant not only with people, but with 'every living creature that is upon the earth' (Gen 9:10). In our time, the movement of thought called 'process theology' has depicted nature at every level, including that of sub-atomic particles, as responding to God's 'aims' and desiring 'satisfaction' in a cosmic community of relationships;[19] even if we do not want to accept this synthesis of science and religion literally, we may at least find it to be a helpful contemporary myth that tries to find words for the mutual influence between God and the world.

Creation is thus a redemptive act, as God lures on all reality to correspond to His purposes, to reflect the harmony of His vision. Following one of the motifs mentioned above, creation is redemption in the sense of overcoming the waters of chaos. But at the same time the particular redemptive acts of God in human history will have an effect upon creation itself. Whatever relation there may be between God and other parts of His creation, human persons have certainly been given a unique capacity to be sons and daughters of God; so we may believe with the apostle Paul that when human response to God through faith in the Word incarnate in history is complete, this will have a decisive impact upon the redemption of the natural world. When human beings reach the destiny for which they are intended in Christ, the 'universe itself will enter upon the liberty and splendour of the children of God' (Rom 8:19).

This brief theological sketch should make clear why the symbolism of water has resonance on both the level of creation and redemption, concerning both natural phenomena and human history. There is no merely random collection of images here; they refer to the activity and self-disclosure of the God who relates Himself to every dimension of the life of His universe. Baptism into the body of Christ means a new depth of relationship between the believer and Christ; it must also involve a new relationship between the individual believer and the whole community of those who are consciously in covenant partnership with God in Christ (the church—1 Cor 12:13). But further still, in the light of the commitment of the triune God to the body of the cosmos, baptism means a new relation of believers to as yet unredeemed humanity and to our whole natural environment.

Thus, in baptism a person becomes involved in a deeper and new way with the web of loving relationships that God weaves with His whole creation. As John Macquarrie puts it, a sacrament 'focuses' the presence of God that we can find elsewhere; God's presence is not limited to the signs of water, bread, and wine, but we can discern it most clearly there.[20] This means that when the baptismal candidate, or the community that witnesses the baptism, encounters God anew through this particular water, they will be the more aware of the presence of God in other situations where water is involved in birth, conflict, cleansing, journey, or refreshment.

7. The scope of grace

The conveying of grace through created things in baptism, as I have been describing it, has considerable implications for the Baptist claim that baptism has its fullest meaning when believers are involved rather than very young infants. Discussion between those who practise infant baptism and those who practise believers' baptism often seems to get stuck in a dispute about the place of grace on the one hand and faith on the other. One often hears it said that infant baptism recognizes the grace of God, while believers' baptism stresses the faith of the person. I hope to have given a rather different slant on this question by approaching it from the viewpoint of the rooting of baptism in creation.

Baptists should in fact be quite willing to recognize that there are elements of *both* faith and divine grace in the act that is called infant baptism. There is the prevenient grace of God, already at work deep in the being of the child, giving life and wholeness, and enticing it towards a personal response of faith to Himself in due time. There is the faith of parents and the Christian community, supporting and nurturing the child as it grows. Most Baptists will also recognize that the completed sequence of infant baptism and later personal faith in Christ sealed in confirmation constitutes initiation into the church as the body of Christ, and many Baptist churches in Britain do not therefore require baptism of believers in this situation.[21] When salvation is seen as a process or a journey, as the World Council of Churches report *Baptism, Eucharist, and Ministry* urges,[22] many Baptists can readily perceive different combinations of grace and faith at different stages of the journey and can find various ceremonies appropriate to mark the stages.

But for all this, Baptists will find important dimensions of baptism missing in the rite as applied to infants, so that it is hard to use the word baptism with any fulness of meaning. A Baptist will certainly find something lacking in the faith expressed there, as the infant himself or herself can vow no personal allegiance to Christ as Lord. But it is not only faith that lacks fulness. It needs to be understood in ecumenical conversations that a Baptist will also want to say that the scope of *grace* in such a baptism is narrower than in the baptism of believers.

After all, grace is not a kind of supernatural substance that is impartially poured out in different circumstances. It is the gracious coming of God as supremely personal into relationship with His creatures, an encounter in which He is also—through His humility—open to being affected by them and their response to Him. If we understand salvation to be not a momentary event, but a journey of growth, then baptism provides a point within the process when God draws near to transform persons in a special way. Salvation cannot be isolated within the act of baptism (as the variety of Christian experience of conversion testifies), but it can be 'focused' there in the moment when the Christian believer is made part of the covenant community of Christ's disciples. Using an element of His creation, water, God offers an opportunity in baptism for a gracious encounter that is rich in experience and associations.

The five water motifs I have surveyed indicate some of the range of experiences through which God enters into relationship with us in life— experiences of new beginning, cleansing, conflict, crossing boundaries, and refreshment of spirit. These experiences that come from living in God's creation are 'focused' in the event of baptism. Moreover, if that encounter is characterized by love then it will be reciprocal, and in His gracious coming God will open Himself to empathy and feeling with the believer who is offering himself or herself for radical discipleship. It is an event that opens meaning for all who participate in it and that is therefore truly initiatory. Some meaning is grasped by the person being baptized in the moment of the event; much more is grasped in retrospect as the believer looks back to this moment of decisive meeting with the crucified and risen Christ; meaning expands in those who share in the act of baptism as part of the church community. In the case of the baptism of infants, however, there will inevitably be a foreclosing of meaning; because the main participant is a very young infant, the meaning of the grace of God will be mainly limited to the idea (important though it is) of prevenient grace.

8. *The loss of meaning in baptism*

Indeed, it is fairly easy to see how the Christian church has continually narrowed the meaning of baptism. Different traditions have tended to overstress one of the five motifs mentioned above, at the expense of others. For example, the Roman Catholic Church has placed major emphasis upon the second motif, the imagery of cleansing; infant baptism has been defined as a washing away of original sin and (in Augustine's influential view) original guilt. This has enabled the development of a theology in which infants can be the 'proper' subjects of baptism. At the opposite extreme, Baptists have tended to emphasize the aspect of baptism as a boundary marker for believers; they have stressed the fifth motif, a moment of separation from past life and commitment to new kingdom values. Despite the potential of believers' baptism for a richness of meaning, they have sometimes narrowed it to that of 'following Christ through the waters of baptism', a mere phase of obedience on the pilgrim journey.

Protestant churches in the Puritan tradition who baptize infants have usually, following Calvin, seen baptism as a sign of the covenant, and so justified the baptism of infants as bringing families within the covenant community. F. W. Dillistone has argued that this Puritan theology also belongs in the area of 'separation' imagery (what I have designated as the fifth motif), and that it has narrowed the New Testament concept of 'the seal of the Spirit' in baptism to a mere sign, which is too much equivalent to the Jewish sign of circumcision, so losing the dynamic of the presence of the life-giving Spirit.[23]

A Baptist may argue (as I have done above) that only the baptism of believers at a responsible age can adequately draw upon the whole range of water-symbolism and enable the baptismal pool to be the focus for God's creative-redemptive process. However, in this case, Baptists should be more alert than they have been to the width of the range of significance. Exploration of such imagery as 'descent into the womb' may well help Baptists to understand and value the prevenient grace of God, which is involved in the whole nurture of a child in the Christian community before it comes to 'birth' as a morally responsible being, and this may lead them to affirm some of those aspects that are vividly presented in the practice of infant baptism. A reflection upon the strong element of initiation in these motifs may also lead Baptists more consistently to practise the sequence followed in other Christian churches, that a person must be baptized before sharing in the Eucharist.

In considering the narrowing of the significance of baptism, perhaps the extreme case is those who are suspicious of any 'sacramentalism', and who argue that baptism is merely an optional outward ceremony symbolizing an inward grace. They view baptism as just one way of bearing witness to having received salvation. Some may argue here that ritual washings were simply part of Jewish culture, and so the baptism of Jesus should not be given normative status within the life of the church thereafter; after all, it may be pointed out, Jesus himself apparently never baptized. In reply, we may suggest that the whole of the Pauline insight into salvation, being identified with the body of Christ in death and resurrection, relies upon the baptismal metaphor (e.g. Rom 6:1-6); and it is hard to see how one could be meaningful without the other. However, we may also point to the location of baptism within the whole scene of creation as we have been considering it. This surely confirms the centrality of the rite to human renewal. The character of baptism as a 'creation symbol' gives it a universality; the archetypal symbols of immersion, sprinkling, and washing with water are embedded so deeply within the human consciousness that there is something 'given' about a water ritual, and a worshipping community is bound to be impoverished if it attempts to do without this creation-redemption sacrament.

9. Baptism, authority, and the purpose of God

Sacraments can, however, carry overtones of power with them. Baptists cannot help but notice that at times in past history, the practice of infant baptism has been misused to support hierarchical structures of authority in church and state. When it was thought that infants must be baptized to grant them salvation and entrance to heaven, then those who had the right of baptizing naturally had a powerful sanction to exercise and a means of control over people. Believers' baptism underlines a final allegiance to Christ alone, though also affirming that this allegiance is not worked out as a private individual, but within the whole *polis* or human community. Believers' baptism is entrance to church membership, which among Baptists (and other dissenting groups arising from the Radical Reformation) is always understood to carry responsibilities of active discipleship. The final authority in a local church is the rule of Christ among his disciples, the presence of the risen Lord who has the 'crown rights of the redeemer.' Human authority consists in the responsibility of all the church members, gathered in church meeting, to find the mind and purpose of Christ for their life and mission.

In coming to their consensus, the members of the church will draw upon such resources as their spiritual gifts, the counsel of other churches, and the insights of a trusted leadership; but they retain the responsibility of making a decision together about what they believe to be the will of Christ. Though Baptists might be surprised to have it so described, their view of the church meeting is therefore quite sacramental[24] and is rooted in a conviction about grace in creation. They expect the Spirit of God to take something material and earthy (their own bodies, gathered together) and use it for a divine-human encounter, for a means of grace. As in the communion bread, the participants in this meeting expect to 'discern the body of Christ' (1 Cor 11:29). The initiation into the body of Christ received in baptism is continued in Lord's Supper *and* church meeting; indeed, in many early Baptist churches the minute book of the church meeting was kept in a drawer under the communion table. Immersion into the death and resurrection of Christ in baptism is to be renewed in eucharistic celebration and in corporate decision making about community lifestyle and service in the world.

Placing the church meeting of the baptized within the perspective of creation also brings a further insight: how decisions are made. While freedom is safeguarded by the mechanism of a democratic vote, the point is not for one block of voters to defeat another or for a majority to oppress a minority voice. It is to perceive the purpose of Christ among the members of his body. But the question then arises as to what it really means to 'find the mind of Christ' in his body, and here a theology of identification with the 'body' of Christ through baptism in the whole context of creation can help.

All too often, and not only among Baptists, the purpose of God for His people is understood to be a fixed programme like a kind of pre-existing divine 'blueprint' or game plan. In the particular context of a Baptist church meeting, the result may be that when members believe they have found the divine 'plan', those who have not voted for a certain course of action may feel effectively excluded; it seems their views are of no account. It is certainly not only those who practise infant baptism who can, as mentioned above, misuse authority in the baptized community. But baptism should point us towards a deeper kind of involvement with the God who has taken on the cosmos as His body, and who has therefore opened Himself to include the responsiveness and creativity of all His members. If God is involved, by His free desire, in an organic process of growth with the human and natural community of the world, then while we must seek for the purposes of God as expressed in the incarnate Word of Christ, there is bound to be something open-ended about those purposes. They cannot have the closure of a detailed plan.

This God involves His creation in the forming of His purposes, and to seek His mind also means to contribute to His vision.

In practical terms, even when a decision has been made in a Baptist church meeting, the members will want to go on listening to those who have opposed it or been unhappy with it to gain something from their insights as the decision is worked out in detail in changing circumstances. It also means that while a local meeting of the baptized in Christ cannot be imposed upon by any external authority, it will always be open to listen to the voices of others, aware that it is dependent upon their help in finding the mind of Christ, whether the voices come from wider groupings of churches or from society outside the church.

In baptism, then, the candidate *and* the community find themselves involved in a deeper way in God's relationships with church, human community, and cosmos. The water as an element of creation actually enables that participation to take place, evoking such experiences as birth, cleansing, conflict, journey, and renewal. These motifs are planted deeply in the human awareness of the natural world, but they also belong to the story of God's pilgrimage with His people through history and are finally focused in the life, death, and resurrection of Jesus Christ.

Through this participation, human persons are enabled not only to discern the purposes of God for His universe, but to take a part in shaping them. There is a hint of this in Adrian Mitchell's poem, selected verses from which I began with, for the 'stuff' he celebrates is not only the resources of nature, but what human beings create from it:

> *Dankworth's alto is made of it, most of it,*
> *Scoobdedoo is composed of it*
> *Plastic*
> *I like that stuff*
>
> *Man-made fibres and raw materials*
> *Old rolled gold and breakfast cereals*
> *Platinum linoleum*
> *I like that stuff*[25]

This too is the world that God is humble enough to take and use. This is the world into which He Himself was content to be immersed for our sake.

Notes to Chapter 3

[1]Adrian Mitchell, *Poems* (Jonathan Cape, London, 1969), 'Four for Children', Poem 2, verses 1, 4, 5, 12, pp. 47-49. In reprints, this poem is now called 'Stufferation'.

[2]F. W. Dillistone, *Christianity and Symbolism* (Collins, London, 1955), p. 187.

[3]E.g. 'The Sumerian Paradise Myth of Enki and Ninhursag' in James B. Pritchard, *Ancient Near Eastern Texts Relating to the Old Testament*, 2nd Edition (Princeton University Press, New Jersey, 1955), pp. 38-9.

[4]C. G. Jung, *Symbols of Transformation*, Complete Works of Jung, Vol. 8, transl. R. F. C. Hull (Routledge and Kegan Paul, London, 1956), pp. 218-19.

[5]E.g. Ezek 16:1-7; Hos 11:1-4; Isa 1:1-3; 63:8-10; Isa 42:14, cf.

[6]Isa 45:10; 66:7-9.

[7]See Aubrey R. Johnson, *Sacral Kingship in Ancient Israel*, Second Edition (University of Wales Press, Cardiff, 1967), pp. 128ff.

[8]See G. R. Beasley-Murray, *Baptism in the New Testament* (Macmillan, London, 1963), p. 26.

[9]Cyril of Jerusalem, *Catacheses Mystagogicae* II.4.

[10]cit. Dillistone, *Christianity and Symbolism*, p. 186.

[11]The key text is Leviticus 17:11. For further explanation see Paul S. Fiddes, *Past Event and Present Salvation. The Christian Idea of Atonement* (Darton, Longman and Todd, London, 1989), pp. 61-82.

[12]See N. Kiuchi, *The Purification Offering in the Priestly Literature. Its Meaning and Function*. JSOT Supplement Series 56 (Sheffield Academic Press, 1987), pp. 65-6.

[13]*The Scroll of the Rule*, III.4-6; A. Dupont-Sommer, *The Essene Writings from Qumran*, transl. G. Vermes (Blackwell, Oxford, 1961), pp. 76-7.

[14]Titus 3:5; Eph 5:26; Heb 10:22; perhaps John 13:5; cf. Rev 7:14.

[15]Ps 105:40-1; 94:8; 78:15-16; Isa 43:20; 44:3; 48:21; Deut 8:15.

[16]Raymond E. Brown, *The Gospel According to John I-XII*, The Anchor Bible (Chapman, London, 1966), pp. 179-80, 327-9.

[17]Beasley-Murray, in *Baptism in the New Testament*, speaks similarly of baptism as a 'trysting place': p. 305.

[18]Ps 19:1-4; 29:5-6; 96:11-12; 98:7-8; 104:26; Rom 8:19-22.

[19]See e.g. J. B. Cobb and D. R. Griffin, *Process Theology: An Introductory Exposition* (Christian Journals, Belfast, 1977), pp. 63-80.

[20]John Macquarrie, *Principles of Christian Theology*, Revised Edition (SCM, London, 1977), p. 449.

[21]While this openness is also found among Baptists in the American Baptist Convention and Baptists in Holland, Italy, and Sweden, many other Baptist

Unions outside Britain do require members and communicants to be baptized as believers.

[22]*Baptism, Eucharist, and Ministry: Faith and Order Paper 111* (World Council of Churches, Geneva, 1982), p. 4.

[23]Dillistone, *Christianity and Symbolism*, pp. 202-6.

[24]I owe this observation to a Church of England colleague, Dr. Timothy Bradshaw.

[25]Adrian Mitchell, 'Four for children', op. cit., p. 48.

4

Baptism as a Political Act

BRIAN HAYMES

1. New humanity, new morality

The New Testament often employs terms of sharp contrast when speaking of the Christian life. Johannine writings include the imagery of moving from darkness to light (1 John 1:5-7) or from death to life (1 John 3:14). Paul writes of being buried and raised with Christ (Rom 6:3-4). He asserts that when anyone is in Christ there is a new creation (2 Cor 5:17). All the New Testament writers presuppose that something critically new has happened for the world in the life, death, and resurrection of Jesus.

Christian baptism proclaims this conviction. The Son of the Father, baptized in the Jordan, has offered a life of perfect submission to the purposes of God, even to death. His baptism is followed by the struggle in the wilderness, the proclamation of the Kingdom of God in words and actions, the conflicts with the various forms that sin takes, until he comes to the cross and the experience of God-forsakenness (Luke 12:50). But in the life, death, and resurrection of Jesus, with the consequent outpouring of the Holy Spirit on all flesh, a new age dawns. The Kingdom, yet to be complete, is nevertheless established. A new humanity is being called into being in Christ. The life of the world may seem to go on much as usual but, in fact, there is something crucially different. The resurrection of humankind has begun in the raising up of Jesus.

To be baptized into Christ is to share the new humanity God is calling into being. It is to belong to a company whose life and order is not marked by ancient divisions (Gal 3:28). It is to be a new people of God:

> But you are a chosen race, a royal priesthood, a dedicated nation, a people claimed by God for his own, to proclaim the glorious deeds of him who has called you out of darkness into his marvellous light. Once you were not a people at all; but now you are God's people. Once you were outside his mercy; but now you are outside no longer (1 Pet 2:9-10).

The turning point for the whole creation is the resurrection of Jesus. A future is created 'which contextualizes and shapes the Christian life as an endeavor taking place between Pentecost and Parousia'.[1]

It is quite evident that the New Testament recognizes that the new life in Christ has moral consequences for the believer. The life of the Christian is assumed to be different from that of other first-century contemporaries (Col 3:1-17). The resurrection is the key, but it makes for a variety of emphases in different contexts. For example, if it is the thought of the present new life in Christ that is uppermost in the apostle Paul's mind, then that leads to the realization that certain pagan practices are incompatible with belonging to Christ (1 Cor 6:15). At other times the thought of the immanent return of Christ is so dominant that it shapes all thought about present behaviour (Rom 13:11ff). And even where the recommended behaviour looks very much like moral codes shared by most people in the New Testament era, the basic appeal for such response is not on the basis of some commonly agreed morality, but to the new life in Christ. As was the case with God's ancient people, so now Christians are called to be godly, holy, Christlike. Being baptized has moral consequences.

Christian behaviour is described in the New Testament often enough in terms of personal ethics. But that is not the limit of New Testament ethics and an understanding of the life in Christ. Baptism is an act with consequences for social ethics. Indeed it would not be going too far to suggest that baptism is an event with political significance.

This claim relates directly to what God has done in Christ Jesus. For example, not a little emphasis in contemporary British Baptist life is put on the importance of 'accepting Jesus Christ as my personal Lord and Saviour'. The intensity of personal relationship with Jesus is thus properly and gratefully celebrated. It is an important feature of an evangelical understanding of the Christian life, a life marked by the joy that belongs to the Kingdom. But the undoubted strength of this personal centre of faith may be overburdened. It surely is if salvation is understood only in individual terms. The New Testament affirms not only that God has done in Christ something for your life and mine, but that the salvation of God is of cosmic significance (Eph 1:20-23; Col 1:14-20). Often this emphasis is made using the apocalyptic imagery current in the forms of Judaism in the New Testament era, and this can read strangely to us. But one particular aspect germane to our concern is what the gospel has to say about Christ and the Powers.

2. Confronting the Powers in baptism

The language of power and the Powers is prevalent in the New Testament.[2] The terms used are not always precise in their meaning, and a considerable body of literature has grown around questions of interpretation.[3] Speaking very generally, there are on the one hand those who argue that the Powers are objectively real as supernatural beings, angels, spiritual beings that are part of the divine but fallen creation. On the other hand, there are others who refer to the Powers as the 'interiority' of institutions, the evil residing not first outside us but within.[4] Whatever stance one takes on such questions, there can be little doubt in the first or twentieth century of the reality of evil and its power to corrupt and destroy.

It is at least plausible to suggest that when Paul spoke of principalities and powers, he held together the thought of the spiritual cosmic powers in creation and the structures or systems of our earthly existence. The concept of the Powers as the structures or system of creation is one profitably explored by H. Berkhof and J. H. Yoder.[5] They suggest that since the only creation we know is a fallen one, the Powers will have negative aspects, but that this 'original sin' should not blind us to any 'original righteousness' that is also theirs. There can be no life, no community, without order and structure. Complete randomness would be indistinguishable from chaos. Thus the Powers were part of the fundamentally good creation (Col 1:15-17). They are God's regularity, order, and system that make the creation a living developing phenomenon. But in the fallen state of our humanity we experience the Powers both positively, as making for life, and negatively, as being oppressive, even tyrannical. The Powers that were intended to serve God's liberating purposes can become despotic. Even so, they do not stand entirely independent of the sovereign purpose of God and of His salvation in Christ.

This can be drawn out a little by reflecting on the baptismal liturgy. In many traditions, including the Baptist, the candidates are called upon to confess the faith of the church. In the most recent book of prayers and orders of worship created by British Baptists, one question that may be put to the baptismal candidate is: 'Do you turn from sin, renounce evil, and intend to follow Christ?'.[6] This reflects an earlier tradition where the formal renouncing of evil and turning from its paths and power is a

crucial feature of the understanding of baptism. It is into this new life
that the candidate is baptized.

In the Baptist tradition, it is usual for the candidate to be totally immersed in water. Here too is powerful symbolism, for water may express
cleansing and so life, but it also signifies the chaos that is only held back
by the creative power of God. Water uncontrolled can be destructive,
chaotic. It can take life as much as sustain it. The very act of plunging
a candidate under the surface expresses the deep threat that is there to
our life. People die by drowning. Some people, fearful of water, find it
hard to confess the faith in this way. Generally, for pastoral reasons, ministers work hard to set the candidates' fears aside. We surround them
with care and tell them that the water is warm and that everything will
be all right. Might not something be restored to baptism by keeping the
water running, cold, such as takes breath away, like those powers that
would overwhelm us all were it not for the work of God? Paul speaks of
our being buried with Christ (Rom 6:4). Our old self is laid in the tomb
with Jesus. Baptism is saying 'You too are dying here', sharing the experience of Holy Saturday, waiting upon the resurrection from the dead. In
the plunging below the waters the hostile powers are confronted, and the
shock effect of it all is not apart from baptism's meaning. The pool
represents the tomb.

3. Structures and oppression

Yoder suggests that in thinking of the Powers, 'We have . . . an inclusive
vision of religious structures (especially the religious undergirdings of
stable ancient and primitive societies), intellectual structures (ologies and
isms), moral structures (codes and customs), political structures (the
tyrant, the market, the school, the courts, race, and nation).'[7] Three
particular illustrations will, I believe, help us grasp this perspective.

First, take the issue of peace and government. It is generally held that
the first responsibility of those in government is to defend and protect the
State. Thus armies and police forces are formed and employed. These are
part of the well-being of the State, keeping peace and order. It might be
argued that the *Pax Romana* illustrates the benefits of this form of power.
By force, threat, and deterrence the Roman army kept peace in the
Empire and gave thereby a measure of security and order to its citizens.
If the alternative is anarchy, then such a peace is much to be desired. But

peace based on force, coercion, and threat is a means of oppression and a long way from what the Bible calls *shalom*. Military order can become militarism, a totalitarian control of citizens by the State for the State. It can lead those in power to argue for acts that would otherwise be unjust, for example, in the suggestion that it is better that one should die than the nation be destroyed. A military peace, such as the much vaunted *Pax Romana*, is almost invariably oppressive and, in the name of stability, freedom is betrayed and much injustice done. Imperial systems function to the benefit of the centre, but at the inevitable cost to the weak and marginal.[8]

Second, a society that is utterly amoral would have the greatest difficulty in maintaining itself as a community. All societies need some basis of shared values, or confusion will result. So corporate strength is received in moral codes and customs. We are moral beings, and the end of morality would be, perhaps, the end of us all. But, at the same time, it is obvious that an unresponsive, unreflective morality enshrined in a code of unqualifiable absolutes legalistically applied can become a curse. Is this not what Paul is arguing can happen with the gracious gift of Torah? Morality reduced to moralism can be oppressive, leaving the individual virtually without any freedom and in need of liberation. Law without grace can become demonic.[9] It can take a woman caught in the act of adultery and stone her to death (John 8:3-11).

For the third illustration, let us take the case of formal theology, the belief content of any religion. Christianity has been particularly blessed in its historical development by the various theological systems devised to commend and explain the Faith. Great intellects have shaped impressive accounts of Christian doctrine, accounts with an orderliness that is at once compelling and beautiful.

But lesser souls, with tighter minds and narrower vision, can corrupt the sensitive, searching, humble faith in God that lies behind these endeavours by making more of them than was ever intended. Thus, champions emerge on behalf of Thomism or Calvinism, some virtually idolizing the structure and ready to defend it against all attacks. In this way, an expression of the Faith becomes a means of identification and exclusion. The evangelical understanding of the truth of the gospel can be reduced to 'evangelicalism', the catholic tradition to 'catholicism'. These theologies can be seen as part of the rich and varied tradition of understanding the faith. But when they are absolutized, then, under these banners Christians have killed one another. Partial and particular expressions of the Faith have been turned into party labels. Even the noblest of theologies can be turned into a demonic tool of oppression.

These illustrations—and there could be many more—are all encompassed in the notion of idolatry. The Powers, so necessary as the structures or systems of our life in creation, can get above themselves and demand a loyalty and devotion that belongs to God alone. The Powers are not inherently bad, but they have often overstepped themselves, and instead of being expressions of God's liberating and creative purpose have become destructive of life and community. If any further illustration is needed, then recall how pride of nation became a particular form of nationalism in Germany and led to the idolatry of Nazism.

The world therefore needs the Powers in creation, but also salvation from the Powers. If what God has done in the cross of Christ merits the word salvation, then God must have not dealt simply with my personal sin, so that 'I with my saviour am happy and blessed', but He must also deal with the Powers. It is important to grasp that Christ is proclaimed Lord over the Powers both by reason of what was accomplished in the cross and also because of his significance in creation.

> In him everything in heaven and on earth was created, not only things visible but also the invisible orders of thrones, sovereignties, authorities and powers: the whole universe has been created through him and for him. (Col 1:16)

Whether they be angels, spiritual beings, or earthly forms that the Powers have taken, all are under this primary lordship of Christ in creation.

But the creation is fallen. So in what way are the Powers brought into the redemptive purposes of Christ? What has Christ done? The church has used a variety of metaphors in its history to explicate Christ's work of atonement in God's salvation. With reference to the Powers, the theme of *Christus Victor* has been most prevalent. But still the questions remain: What kind of victory is this, given the fact that the Kingdom has not yet come in its fulness? And by what means did Christ win the victory, given the fact of the cross?

Here Berkhof helpfully summarizes what God has done in Christ with regard to the Powers under three headings:[10] (1) Christ has made a public spectacle of them, bringing to light their true nature. (2) This unmasking of the Powers is already their defeat as Christ challenged them and showed his strength over them. (3) Thus the Powers are 'disarmed', and nothing they can do can ever separate us from the love of the Christlike God for us.

4. *Victory as exposing the Powers*

Clearly, the Powers are not yet totally under the control and rule of Christ. The New Testament witnesses knew this to be true in their own painful experiences. But the faith they proclaimed is that the Powers are exposed and unmasked. This is expressed in the imagery of warfare, when it is affirmed that they are defeated Powers over which Christ has achieved a decisive victory. The Powers, ultimately to be captive to Christ's purposes, are part of the royal triumphal procession (Col 2:15). They are not destroyed but brought again to their proper role and purpose in the will of God.

After all, the language of victory and triumph can sound somewhat empty in the light of the world as we know it. If Christ really has won a victory, its effects nevertheless appear to be limited. To fail to acknowledge the eschatological tension within the New Testament is to misunderstand the nature of Christ's work, which in itself can lead to a discipleship that, in triumphalism, bypasses the suffering that must still be borne in the service of the Kingdom.

In what way, then, has Christ overcome the Powers? Christ broke the power of the Powers by exposing their pretensions and thereby disarming them. Thus, in his earthly ministry, Jesus confronted the Powers with his words and deeds. For example, he challenged the oppressive legalism that went with Sabbatarianism. He healed on the Sabbath Day, in keeping with the life of the Kingdom. Again, he did not condone the woman taken in adultery, but by his own response exposed the attitude of those who charged her and would seek to destroy her and him by their appeal to law. As we have seen, religion, morality, and intellect can all become means of oppression, sources of slavery, from which God wants to bring liberation. Jesus was ready to identify these oppressive corruptions for what they were. His challenge to them begins with their identification.

But, more significantly, the gospel story goes on to tell of Jesus' submission in two senses. Clearly, in the story of his betrayal, trials, scourging, and crucifixion, Jesus submits to the works of the Powers. He is crucified by religious power and the 'justice' of the *Pax Romana*. The Prince of this world has his hour. Jesus becomes a victim of the sin of the world, killed by the power of the Powers. But in another sense, no one takes his life from him. He lays it down of his own accord. He may be the victim of the destructive forces, but they do not destroy him because he refuses to submit to them in an ultimate sense. There is no power over one whose total loyalty is in submission to the will of God. In this way the Powers' pretension to absoluteness is exposed, and they are seen for what they are.

The real sin of the Powers is idolatry. They operate as if they had an independence of the divine rule, as if they could lay a claim on human-kind that properly belongs only to God. Jesus submits himself to their work, only to show their real but partial power. Only in the service of God is there perfect liberty. By his death on the cross Jesus reveals what the powers are, what they can and will do, and exposes them as impos-ters. So a victory is won in the cross. The cycle of sin and its power is broken. The salvation God brings includes the exposing and therefore the redeeming of the Powers; and it is achieved, not in spite of, but through the death of His Son.

The New Testament witnesses proclaim that all this has happened. There is a once-for-all victory won in the cross of Christ, and though it may be that the Powers are not yet totally submissive to the Lord, none-theless God's salvation is assured. God's raising of the crucified is His great 'Yes' to the life and death of Christ. A new age has dawned. The hope of new creation has drawn near as God's salvation and the comple-tion of all creation has come out of the future into our present with challenge and choice.

5. Baptism, confession, and politics

There is then no escaping the sense of crisis that goes with the gospel. If the truth has been exposed for all to see, the gospel is not just about whether some things are believed as matters of fact, but whether a new life is to be lived, whether there is a new way to be followed. The claim is that Jesus, in his life and death on the cross, has confronted and dis-armed those Powers that hold our humanity in thrall. This Jesus, once despised and rejected, God has raised from death. He is Lord, and his lordship will have no end.

That Jesus is Lord is the fundamental baptismal confession. To be baptized into Christ, in the name of the triune God, is to be baptized into a realm where the Powers are exposed for what they are and where new possibilities for liberated living emerge. The pool represents not only tomb; it also represents womb. To be baptized is, among other things, to be drawn by the grace of God, through faith in Jesus Christ, into the new order of hope and salvation. Here in baptism an absolute loyalty to Christ is confessed. In this sense baptism is political, carrying considerable ethical significance, raising as it does basic questions of identity, allegiance, and obedience. If Jesus Christ is Lord, then he is to be followed. Our values and goals will be his, and not just those of the society and ethos that have their own power to form us. The exposure of the powers is repeated in the confession of baptism.

One of the most celebrated illustrations of this point is that of the Barmen declaration of the 'Confessing Church' in the Germany of the 1930s. With the immense power and influence of the Nazi machine, many Germans, not least in the churches, were drawn into a nationalism and racism that were an open challenge to the gospel. But there were others who declared that

> Jesus Christ, as he is testified to us in Holy Scripture, is the one Word of God which we are to hear, which we are to trust and obey in life and death. We repudiate the false teaching that the church can and must recognize yet other happenings and powers, personalities and truths, as divine revelation alongside this one Word of God, as a source of her preaching.[11]

The consequences of affirming, preaching, and living such a declaration of loyalty to Jesus Christ were quickly seen to be enormous, not least by those in power. They were bound to respond. They argued that it is, after all, the duty of the State to keep good order for the flourishing of life of all the citizens. They could even invoke scripture in their support, for example, Romans 13. But here is an illustration of the Powers in their fallen state laying claim to what belonged ultimately to God. To live the life of the baptized was to stand against this great evil, even if necessary to death. In 1945 Reinhold Niebuhr wrote,

While modern secularism speaks naively about the sociological source of conscience, the most effective opponents of tyrannical governments today are, as in the past, those who can say 'We must obey God rather than man'. Their resolution is possible because they have a vantage point from which they can discount the pretensions of daemonic Caesars, and from which they can defy malignant power as embodied in a given government.[12]

Two memories from the Baptist Assembly in London in 1992 come to mind. David Quinney-Mee, a missionary in El Salvador, spoke of the mass poverty, the military oppression, and other effects of the civil war that had torn the country apart. He spoke of how, in the face of this, the churches had come to work together. The reality they faced was not in the question of how denominations can cooperate but how they can live together in the presence of the poor. He spoke of the many who had died in the struggles and of the experience amid such suffering of being at the foot of the cross. This, he said, 'is the place that engenders Christian commitment and hope, as people live between life and death'. He told of the Christian church living out its costly calling and being a sign of hope.

A different illustration came from someone who spoke about a credit union being set up by the Salford Urban Mision in the United Kingdom. The speaker described how the union is run by local people who thereby learn to manage their own finances and keep free from the loan sharks; so 'it is people, in the community caring for one another; it has brought hope to a large number of people'. The story continued with an account of a man who had seen the risen Christ at work in this piece of service, and who had subsequently been baptized.

6. Baptism into a new ethical community

Baptism is not just an act of personal commitment to the One who saves me from my sin. By our baptism into Christ we belong to a new community—the church—that ponders, celebrates, and continues the story of salvation. We receive the gift of other Christians, members together in the body of Christ. There are no private deals with Jesus. The New Testament knows nothing of solitary religion, for all the essential personal nature of faith. It is always faith expressing itself in relationship, in the church. And the consequence of serving a different Lord from others is that the church will be, in some sense, an alternative society. Its members will not live apart from the world but within it as salt and light, witnesses to the Kingdom of God.

Some recent debates in Christian ethics have led to a new emphasis on the church as a corporate body and a community of moral formation. One of the products of the Enlightenment was 'the autonomous individual', a free person who was a moral centre of heroic will. The burden of responsible choice, of deciding the right and the good, rested not on 'authorities' external to the individual, but each of us must choose as the free persons we are. In this view of the person, we may listen to others, to the church, to God, but the choice is ours. That is our freedom.

But more recently others have asked whether this is the whole substance of our moral being. They have recalled classic debates about morality as 'virtue' and as the cultivation of good habits. They have reminded us that our moral judgments and sense are shaped by the communities to which we belong, communities where we find our identity in shared history and values. The church, in particular, might be understood therefore as 'a community of character.'[13]

Identifying, exposing, and resisting the oppressive influence of the Powers is a corporate act. The church's ethical response is part of its witness to the claims of Christ the Lord. We are baptized into a community that seeks not for its ways and will to be moulded by the fashions of present or the past, but for its mind and nature to be transformed by Christ and in Christ. The church goes on working at its ethical response in keeping with the lordship of Christ. It is not a matter only of seeking some personal transformation, on the basis of which we set about changing the world. Nor is it a matter only of a full frontal assault on the structures of our society that oppress. It is both of these. The Christian, being transformed by the grace of Christ, resists the Powers and in company with others affirms a different perspective, a world in which Christ is Lord.

7. A new community, but not a sect

A criticism often made against the argument advanced here involves its supposed sectarian nature. Usually, academic discussions about 'sects' involve distinctions drawn between 'sect' and 'church' as two religious social forms. Such distinctions cover institutional sense, hierarchies, and relationships with the rest of humankind in its common life. But popular notions of 'sects' also imply social and moral separation from the main body of humankind and religious separation from other believers, usually on the grounds of doctrinal and moral purity.[14] The natural home for the sect is the desert, as a separated community way outside the mainstream of corporate human life.

This essay has argued that this ought not to be the stance of the Christian church. The understanding of baptism argued for here sees the baptized as, on the one hand, one with all humankind in its 'fallenness' and need, struggling with the Powers, subject to sin and death. But, on the other hand, the baptized have come to share the life of the triune God, living by the grace that found focus in the life, death, and resurrection of Jesus and the gift of the Holy Spirit. The Christlike God is calling a new humanity into being. Yet those who share this life are but members of the old humanity now participating by grace in the redeeming purposes of God. The church is composed of sinners, those who have by grace responded to the call of God into the new life in Christ. Its members in that sense are different from those who have not so responded. But they have not yet arrived at the Kingdom's goal.

So this view of the Christian life in no way seeks to diminish the eschatological tension inherent in the gospel. The church waits for the completion of all things in Christ. It does so in quiet trust of God's mercy without presuming either that its members are special in God's eyes or that grace is so cheap it can be taken for granted. So Christians are called to serve the present age, living out all their natural and social responsibilites in the world, but doing that in the hope of the coming Kingdom. There may be all manner of temptations to self-righteousness, spiritual pride, and religious bigotry, but these are corruptions of the Christian calling to be salt and light for all the world.

The sectarian spirit of exclusiveness is not part of the life of the baptized. The particular identity of Christians does not remove them from the general identity of human beings with all the moral and political implications that go with sharing a common life. For all that they may follow a different Lord, Christians are not called to sectarianism as a form of negative separateness. To be baptized into Christ is to be baptized into one who, at the Jordan and the cross, totally immersed himself in human life. We remember that the form of his death was political. He was not crucified for forming a small group of followers who shared an interest in 'spiritual truths'. The implications of his teaching and living could not be discarded to the safety of the desert by the powers of the day. They, at least, recognized that he implied more than that.

In the chapel of the Northern Baptist College, Manchester, there is a mural that pictures the life of Manchester through its buildings and institutions. There you can see the banks, the commercial offices, the hospitals, the university, the council flats, the city offices, the churches— all that makes up the life of this modern city. The artist has delicately shot the tapestry through with silver and gold thread so that when the light shines on it it is transformed. In this way, those who come to worship in chapel have the city kept before their eyes. There is no escaping the context of worship and the place where we are called to be disciples in hope that even this all too-human city might know the *shalom* that belongs to the city of God.

8. Confession and exposing the Powers

We are now more than halfway through the 'Decade of Evangelism'. Much of the language employed, understandably enough, centres upon the growth of the church. But the challenge of the Kingdom goes beyond that. We are still oppressed by Powers who do not yet submit to the rule of Christ. So, for political and economic reasons, half the world is hungry;and thousands die each day to serve the gods of economic theories that favour the strong. What would it be like to be members of communities that had 'named' the powers of advertising and consumerism and were being freed, together, to live lives of *koinonia* (fellowship) in the Spirit? Further, legitimate national defence can become militarism where vast resources, economic and human, are used to perpetuate policies of fear and death. And only slowly, not least in our churches, do we realize the demonic power of sexism whereby women are denied the fulness of their humanity, sometimes in the name of religion. We wrestle not against flesh and blood, but we must wrestle with these and other issues of oppression if we are to be true to our calling in Christ.

All of this is not to see the world as a place of unrelieved despair, oppression, and wickedness. The story the church lives by and goes on telling is of a gracious God intent on making all things new. It is of the work of God in a real world. As Yoder expressed it:

The Powers have been defeated not by some kind of cosmic hocus-pocus, but by the concreteness of the cross; the impact of the cross upon them is not the working of magical words nor the fulfilment of a legal contract calling for the shedding of innocent blood, but the sovereign presence within the structures of creaturely orderliness, of Jesus the kingly claimant and of the church who herself is a structure and a power in society. Thus the historicity of Jesus retains, in the working of the church as she encounters the other power and value structures of her history, the same kind of relevance the man Jesus had for those whom he served until they killed him.[15]

That the church exists, telling the story of God's ways with us, of Christ's overcoming of the Powers—all of this is of crucial importance. There can be few things more vital than that such a church exists and that those who are its members, baptized into Christ, lay claim to Christ's victory and live in his lordship with all the political consequences that follow from this confession.

Notes to Chapter 4

[1]Philip LeMasters, *Discipleship for All Believers* (Herald Press, Scottdale, 1992), p. 18.

[2]Walter Wink, *Naming the Powers. The Language of Power in the New Testament* (Marshall-Pickering, Basingstoke, 1988), p. 7. The passages of special concern are Rom 8:38ff; 1 Cor 2:8; 15:24-26; Eph 1:20ff; 2:1ff; 6:12; Col 1:6; 2:8-20.

[3]For example: G. B. Caird, *Principalities and Powers* (Clarendon Press, Oxford, 1956); G. H. C. MacGregor, 'Principalities and Powers. The Cosmic Background of Paul's Thought', *New Testament Studies* 1 (1954), pp. 17-28; E. Gordon Rupp, *Principalities and Powers* (Epworth Press, London, 1952); Hendrikus Berkhof, *Christ and the Powers* (Herald Press, Scottdale, 1962); John Howard Yoder, *The Politics of Jesus* (Eerdmans, Grand Rapids, 1972); A. H. van den Heuven, *These Rebellious Powers* (Friendship Press, New York, 1965); W. Carr, *Angels and Principalities* (Cambridge University Press, Cambridge and New York, 1982); Walter Wink, *Naming the Powers*, op.cit.; Wink, *Unmasking the Powers. The Invisible Forces that Determine Human Existence* (Fortress Press, Philadelphia, 1986); Wink, *Engaging the Powers. Discernment and Resistance in a World of Domination* (Fortress Press, Philadelphia, 1992).

[4]Walter Wink, *Naming the Powers*, op. cit., p. 104.

[5]Yoder, *The Politics of Jesus*, op. cit.; Berkhof, *Christ and the Powers*, op. cit.

[6]*Patterns and Prayers for Christian Worship. A Guidebook for Worship Leaders*. The Baptist Union of Great Britain (Oxford University Press, Oxford, 1991), p. 101.

[7]Yoder, op.cit., p. 145.

[8]The issue of *pax* and *shalom* is illustrated in the contrasting arguments of the Church of England report *Peacemaking in a Nuclear Age* (Church House Publishing, London, 1988) and *Theology Against the Nuclear Horizion*, edited by Alan Race (SCM Press, London, 1988); in the former, the need for nuclear deterrence is argued for on the basis that coercion is part of the concept of *pax,* but in the latter *shalom* is interpreted theologically as a critique of *pax,* going beyond the absence of war to a christologically inspired vision.

[9]There is little evidence to suggest that Jesus was very interested in morals: see N. P. Harvey, *The Morals of Jesus* (Darton, Longman and Todd, London, 1991)

[10]Berkhof, op. cit., pp. 36-46

[11]From the first article of the Barmen Declaration; translation quoted is from E. H. Robertson, *Christians against Hitler* (SCM, London, 1962), pp. 48-52.

[12]Reinhold Niebuhr, *The Children of Light and the Children of Darkness,* (Nisbet, London, 1945), p. 60.

[13]This is the title of a book by Stanley Hauerwas who explores this theme: Hauerwas, *A Community of Character* (University of Notre Dame Press, London, 1981). The debate in ethics is briefly but well summarised by Robin Gill in *Christian Ethics in Secular Worlds* (T. & T. Clark, Edinburgh, 1991), ch. 1.

[14]There may be, of course, other sociological forces at work. See H. R. Niebuhr, *The Social Sources of Denominationalism* (Meridian Books, New York, 1975).

[15]Yoder, op. cit., p. 162.

5

Baptism and the Identity of Christian Communities

RICHARD KIDD

1. Starting from a muddle?

On issues of baptism, whether in principle or practice, Christians of the late twentieth century inherit what seems to be a distressingly complex muddle. The question facing believers of every tradition and, not least, those like myself who own the explicit label 'Baptist', is whether this seeming muddle is inevitably destructive or whether it can become creative for the vitality of the gospel in our time.

The muddle apparently confronting us is not hard to discern. It has a number of well-documented features. There is confusion about the age at which baptism should take place: is it for newborn babies, for children at a particular moment in their development through puberty towards adolescence, or is it strictly for those of 'riper years' who can evidence significant personal testimony to the Christian gospel? Is it by sprinkling or immersion? Are there *any* circumstances under which baptism is repeatable? Is baptism necessary for salvation? Is it primarily about the individual before God, or about the community and its affirmation of faith? These are just some of the confusing questions that spring to mind when baptism is mentioned today.

It is much harder to decide how we might respond to this situation in a creative way. In reply to each of the above questions, there have always been those who bluntly say, 'We are right and others are wrong!' —as if that were the end of it. I do not doubt that there will be many who continue to respond in that way long into the future. For some of us, however—and here I begin to pin my own colours to the mast—that response simply will not do any more! The world is already too racked with pain and conflict to permit Christians the luxury of adding to its fragmentation by internal arguments about baptism. There are, it seems to me, far more significant 'gospel' issues demanding our attention in the world today: issues of justice, reconciliation, human dignity, and community—all of which make disputes about baptism look really rather trivial.

But questions about baptism do not go away. This state of confusion is one of the 'givens' with which we all must work, and a decision about baptism and the meaning it signals is ultimately connected with decisions about priority gospel issues such as those I named above. Is it possible in these ecumenical days to combine a vigorous commitment to a specific baptismal tradition, such as that which Baptists like myself have made to believers' baptism, with a positive affirmation of others who make equally vigorous commitments to very different positions on the spectrum of contemporary views about baptism? What are the options open to those of us who are Baptists?

A first option, one with a significant historical pedigree and practised by many sincere Christians today, is to abandon the practice of baptism altogether. There is evidence to suggest that even Jesus increasingly distanced himself from the practice of baptism as his ministry progressed in order not to detract from the real impact of his teaching by the erecting of ritual barriers, which might contradict the 'fluidity' of the community that gathered around him.[1] I hear the force of the option that calls us to leave the practice of baptism behind and, especially in days when once again it might be easier to argue about baptism than to live as disciples, I feel its challenge—though it is not the option I choose for myself.

A second option is to work towards some form of common statement or principle that will permit assent from the widest possible range of Christians and their respective communions. This has attractions. Something of the kind has been explored by the World Council of Churches over a number of years, a process focused in the *Baptism, Eucharist, and Ministry* statement of 1982.[2] But the official Baptist responses to this document demonstrated very clearly the limitations of this option.[3] We Baptists, because of our ecclesiological tendency to emphasize the autonomy of local congregations, had no real mechanism for making a response anyway; inasmuch as we tried, our offering was little more than a statistical self-analysis revealing the measure of division already amongst us. I am not suggesting that the process called *Baptism, Eucharist, and Ministry* was unimportant for mutual understanding, and I am glad it took place; but, ultimately, I can find little lasting hope in the quest for a common statement. I sense that it is a quest that inevitably gives birth to new communities of dissent and merely perpetuates the fragmentation that historically has caused so much pain and stands in such striking contrast to the authentic spirit of the gospel.

I want, therefore, to explore a third option. It is not an option that can be guaranteed rapidly or dramatically to unravel the global muddle. It is, however, a profoundly Christian option, an option for disciples who are looking for fresh ways to think about themselves and others, and who are content more slowly to chip away at this offensive scar on the visible church. My third option begins with a 'letting go', the kind of letting go that will release people to discover meaning in the diversity of baptismal principles and practices, and that enables them to celebrate that diversity rather than struggle against it.

Doubtless there are several ways of setting about such a process. We might, for example, simply stress the priority of Christian tolerance over our tendency to condemn those we know to 'have it wrong'. That, however, is not enough for me. I want to know if there is a model of the origin and significance of baptismal traditions that actually points towards legitimate diversity, and so helps me to see my own tradition as one amongst many, each with its own significance and integrity. In other words, without giving up my own Baptist convictions about believers' baptism, I want to go beyond the question about who is right and who is wrong!

One way of doing this, the one I propose as a third option, draws on the young but powerful tools of social analysis, and especially those that enable us to investigate the role of rituals or 'signs' in the formation of cultural identity. By taking this option, two things should be achieved. First, it should become clearer why baptism, being tightly bound up with issues of identity, so readily becomes a matter of heated dispute. Second, it should be possible to provide an explanatory framework within which to understand why a living cultural 'text' such as baptism takes on a plurality of lives and rightly becomes 'styled' in radically different ways in different cultural contexts.

If, in addition, it can also be shown that this is how it has always been with Christian faith from the beginning, then I shall have gone some considerable way towards relieving the anxiety that the muddle about baptism inevitably creates. I further hope that the freedom so gained will enable us to experiment more easily with fresh understandings and practices in the diversity of the specific contexts into which we are called to live out the gospel at the present time. I am thinking, not least, of contexts in which more than one baptismal rite is offered within the life of a single worshipping community.

2. Baptism as a living sign

This way of thinking is not especially new; it has been forming over a period of years, represented in theology by the coming together of a number of strands. For example, in the latter decades of the nineteenth century an explosion took place in the detailed study of religions from all over the world. It began with the meticulous documentation of patterns of religious activity in tribal groups and grew in the early twentieth century into a recognizable theological school that took as its starting point the exploration of 'myth and ritual'.[4] What became exciting and provocative for change was the discovery of common 'ritual forms' spanning, as it were, very diverse religious and cultural groups. Baptismal rituals certainly seem to belong amongst such 'forms' and, though various characteristics could be singled out for special mention, it is probably as 'initiation ritual' that baptism can most easily be labelled. There is, it seems, a whole cluster of ritual practices, baptism amongst them, that are designed to initiate and sustain the sense of 'belonging' and to form the building blocks of communal identity. It is no accident, therefore, that in the early years of ecumenical exploration, Christians of many traditions turned to the concept of 'initiation' as a useful point of entry into talk about baptism.[5]

It is, however, through issues of language, which still dominate many branches of the social sciences, that the nature and significance of 'signs' has really come to the fore. This is to use the idea of language in a very broad sense, not limiting it merely to the 'words' we speak, but allowing it to embrace the whole range of codes or 'signs' that we use to convey meaning. Enlarging the idea of language in this way, we can go on to discover strategies and tools with which to explore our rituals, religious practices, doctrines, and celebrations. These are, we might say, all 'texts' that can be 'read', as any written text might be read in the search for meaning. Here my concern is to read what is being articulated by the rite of baptism in each particular culture. What is the meaning of the text 'baptism' in this given setting? What does it say, and how does it say it?

In the very selective comments that follow, I will draw on a range of unnamed sources, from early sociologists such as Durkheim up to the present day. Much of the material here relies on Robert Schreiter's fascinating synthesis of resources in his *Constructing Local Theologies*.[6] In that book he explores models through which to understand the formation of communal identity. Central to his approach is an emphasis on the concept of 'group boundary'; that is, the way we make a boundary by which we separate 'the world of *us*' from 'the world of *them*', sometimes referred to more briefly as the 'internal' and the 'external' worlds.

Often 'primitive' peoples, so-called, are found to have one word for those in their own group that translates something like 'human' or 'person', and a different word for those non-persons outside the group, the barbarians. 'Our society is organized; theirs is chaotic,' they might say. 'Such organization as they have is a threat to ours; even their religious practices are demonic.' I note here with some shame the ease with which I can make connections between this kind of talk and practices in my own religious tradition, practices with which I easily conspire.

Building on this very simple model, we can see how rituals of identity, including rites of passage such as baptism, are essential in the formation and maintenance of culture. Rites of passage enable us to review what it means to be part of a particular culture, what are the responsibilities within it, and how one should act and perceive the world. This is the case at a wedding or a bar mitzvah, and on each occasion the rite is accompanied by a 'sign', which comes to represent in itself the ritual in its entirety. The sign, as it were, becomes the bearer of the message. The sign becomes very potent indeed, and is easily recognisable as a locus of intense religious significance.

So what happens when we begin to think about baptism in these terms? We would need to look at different baptismal rituals and ask how the words, phrases, and actions within them are designed to separate the internal from the external world; how through them the identity of a particular group is reviewed and reinforced. The rituals may be diverse, but in each community the single sign 'baptism' is the bearer of the message.

Many factors can influence the contents of a ritual, and we must try to explore some of the influences that might shape the understanding and practice of baptism. In times of war and persecution, for example, it is not entirely surprising that the awareness of the boundary between 'us' and 'not us' should be considerably strengthened, and crossover made significantly harder. Those who belong to the external world may be wrong, but the fact that they are powerful profoundly shapes what we do.

More intriguing still is an analysis of what happens in present western societies and cultures, where a common assumption is that the external world has no power, whether it be identified as the Third World or 'the unfortunates' in our society. In one sense, it would seem reasonable that under these conditions boundaries could become less important, and that the way could be opened for a new and creative pluralism. In reality, however, people fear the loss of identity that usually goes with a secular kind of pluralism, and they feel an even greater need to erect boundaries as means of creating identity. So in a plural society, where no one cares whether we are Christians or not, it sometimes seems as if there is a drive to work even harder at the issue of identity and to generate the rituals that will sustain it. Some have offered this as an explanation for the recent increased interest in adult baptism amongst all sections of the Christian community. I would have to add something about the enthusiasm at present in my own denomination for developing and sharpening the concept of 'Baptist identity', and I freely admit that I am myself contributing here to that concern.

At this point, however, it might be possible to contrast some secular ideas of 'pluralism', often leading to fearful and defensive responses, with other more productive forms of pluralism that are possible within the vision of Christian believing. There has always been a strong movement amongst Christian traditions to reduce rather than strengthen the height of the boundaries. I am thinking of those traditions, from the gospel parable of the sheep and the goats (Matt 24:31-46), through the boundary-breaking ministries of Saint Francis and his followers to the theology of Dietrich Bonhoeffer and his idea of the 'form of Christ in the world', which find the authentic presence of Christ essentially outside the boundary—in the external world. In this way they actually turn the internal and the external inside out. These traditions offer the possibility of a strong communal identity achieved, not by the height or rigidity of its boundaries, but on an energy generated from its centre—namely, the Christ.

But there is still more to be culled from the theory of signs. The precise meaning of any sign at a particular time is a complicated thing; it is dictated both by its context and its relation to other signs. The result is a process by which meaning is formed, rather, that is, than a fixed meaning given to us with the sign itself. This is why I want to speak of signs as 'living'. Once cut free from an originating context, many different things can happen. The sign we call 'baptism' does not simply carry a pre-given meaning, nor is it uniquely tied to a ritual. It does not have its whole meaning lurking below the surface that can be pierced by a technique such as biblical study or historical reconstruction. Because it 'lives', the sign we call baptism has already generated many independent histories; each points beyond itself, and each bears meaning only in relation to other signs with which it connects.

Returning, then, to the linguistic paradigm with which this section began, the vitality of the sign might be explored by likening its operation to that of metaphor in everyday language. As in metaphor, when what appear to be separate signs come together in relationship, new meaning is born. So it is that the living sign we call baptism is enhanced with fresh meaning in different contexts and properly gives rise to different ritual representations.[7]

3. Some ancient examples

Can I illustrate these motifs at work in the New Testament period itself? Wide-ranging scholarship throughout this century, by its very diversity, suggests that I can. The process by which the sign we call baptism came into being has many facets, and different schools of research place special emphasis on each in differing measure.[8] Each context, however, has a distinct metaphorical power in giving life to the baptismal sign. One context, for example, is Jewish, seen especially in the traditions of ritual washing and purification. Another, related but distinct, belongs to the community at Qumran that produced the writings now called 'the Dead Sea Scrolls'. Considering temple Judaism to be irredeemably polluted, the community's *Manual of Discipline* prescribes a variety of water rituals; but it is not the act alone that is cleansing, rather it is the conjunction of washing and repentance. So the linkage between bathing and penitence is given ritual form in a variety of initiatory as well as repeatable rituals.

By contrast, in a different context, proselyte baptism is used to mark the conversion of Gentiles and so is available strictly on a once-only basis. Though precise connections with Christian origins are hard to prove, points of contact especially through the methods of catechism provide suggestive parallels. Finally, it has not been difficult to draw creative comparisons with some practices in the mystery cults, in which motifs of 'dying and rising' appear to echo familiar themes from Pauline apologetic.

The point is not to argue that Christian baptism has measurable roots in each or any of these sources. Rather it is to show that in its emergence it is these diverse contexts that, from the beginning, produced fertile settings in which baptismal traditions burst into life.

Many would say that the diversity is already present within the New Testament collection of writings; that is, that there is no such thing as the New Testament meaning of baptism anyway. Elements of the diversity are easily named. Connections with the 'baptism of John', associated with Jesus' own baptism, are clear, although the Gospels have difficulty interpreting precisely how this should be read. They are tempted to link this baptism with repentance; but Matthew, clearly aware of the christological implications of such a linkage in the baptism of Jesus, is much more guarded than some.[9] An emphasis on the coming of the Spirit seems to focus on who Jesus is rather than on the baptism itself.

Then there is the uncertainty about whether Jesus baptized any of his followers himself. There is already some ambiguity about this within the body of the Fourth Gospel.[10] In Acts the assumption is that Christians baptized from earliest times.[11] The repentance motif is sustained, but the emphasis is on the act of God and entry into the community. Baptism is 'in the name of Jesus'; it is essentially an act of identification, and the baptizers in some sense represent Jesus in their own ministry.

The Pauline imagery is very varied within itself. There are the images of 'dying and rising', most notably as dying with Christ in immersion and rising to share in the eschatological promise of resurrection. It is important, however, that, though the dying is immediate, the rising remains in promise (Rom 6:5). Elsewhere there is the image of 're-clothing', the putting on of the garment of salvation (Gal 3:27). Elsewhere again there are images primarily suggestive of intitiation into community, the community of a church that itself anticipates the community of the heavenly kingdom (Eph 4:2-6).

As the images are diverse, so undoubtedly were the practices; though, of course, nowhere does the New Testament give a description of a baptismal rite. It has not been difficult, therefore, for scholars to read back intimations of almost any baptismal practice they seek to endorse. Immersing seems essential to make real sense of the Pauline burial imagery. Naked baptism, I suppose, would make best sense of the re-clothing image. There is evidently a connection to the formula 'Jesus is Lord', with its further connection to the imperial context and the formula 'Caesar is Lord' (Rom 10:9). If the Ethiopian is taken as a paradigm, baptism appears to be immediate, without catechism (Acts 8:26-40); and, consistent with the structure of the Roman household, it seems that baptism of the male head of the house led to the baptism of wives and slaves —and possibly children (Acts 16:31-34).

All this signals that the sign was already alive, and alive in a variety of contexts, many of which unfortunately we cannot really begin to identify before the second century and beyond. By then, explanations and practices associated with baptism were diverse and elaborate. On the model offered in the previous section, the metaphorical collision of this sign with other signs and with fresh contexts gives life to ever new meanings and practices. Soon there are immersings and pourings. For some, the temperature and the movement of the water become significant elements in the ritual.[12] Within a relatively short time, Hippolytus, writing from one specific geographical context, describes 'prayers over the water', the 'removal of clothes', a 'pre-baptismal exorcism', a 'threefold baptism' and a 'threefold confession of faith', the 'anointing with holy oil', and much more.[13] By contrast, from an entirely different context, Theodore of Mopsuestia notes a 'signing on the forehead', the presence of a 'godparent', the 'self-immersion' of the candidate by 'bowing under the hand of a priest', the donning of a 'radiant garment' after the baptism, and so on.[14] Vastly different contexts are already generating vastly different ritual forms, each responding to particular cultural settings. It would be hard to say that any one of these developments is 'wrong'; each is fascinating in its own time and place, and each is one part of the many histories of baptism now to be told.

At the core, however, of each of these ritual forms can be discerned the theme of boundary and the formation of cultural identity through the familiarity of the rite. At some places and at some times, the boundaries are evidently high; at other times, they are relatively low. But the vitality of the faith and its representation in the sign we call baptism are absolutely dependent on its ability to respond to each fresh cultural encounter.

4. Some Contemporary Examples

But if this is true of the ancient past, is it not essential that baptism sustain its vitality today in similar ways? What might I say, for example, about the vitality of the sign 'baptism' as it shapes the cultural identity of those who call themselves Baptists in Britain at the present time? It must be acknowledged, of course, that to speak of Baptists is already to embrace a wide spectrum of understanding, from the strongly 'sacra-mental' with its emphasis on the immediate presence and activity of God to the 'merely a picture' with its emphasis on the testimony of the be-liever to an already completed activity of God in conversion—and much inbetween. A majority of Baptist understandings, however, have in com-mon a strong sense of the boundary between 'in' and 'out', the internal and the external. This is often reinforced as baptism is associated with membership of the church community, and as belonging to the commu-nity is associated with belonging to the Kingdom.

It is not hard to imagine times in the Baptist story when this high boundary strategy was of tremendous importance. Through an extended period of the formative years of Baptist tradition, a context of opposition and outright persecution left little alternative. But what about today when the culture we call 'Baptist', and with it the sign we call 'baptism', inter-acts with other strong cultures and signs?

Of primary theological significance I want to name the cultural shift, manifesting itself in a wide range of ways, by which 'humanity' increas-ingly becomes the starting point for analysis and understanding—the shift to anthropology some call it.[15] Potentially this is a shift that enables movement towards a pluralist kind of culture. No longer can a person/ non-person boundary adequately describe the prevailing worldview. Shared humanity precedes religious identity, or any other. But this creates a peculiar crisis for those signs that rely on high boundaries, and the cri-sis shows up at a number of strategic points; most obviously where there is need to respond to an issue of marginalization, or to a challenge from pluralism, not previously part of the cultural agenda. Let me offer three examples by way of illustration.

My first example concerns our response to those who have learning disabilities. Most Baptist practice, with its emphasis on sophisticated cog-nitive responses by baptismal candidates, has traditionally excluded those with severe and even moderate disabilities from participation in the rite we call baptism.[16] Our sign, however, can no longer avoid interaction with other signs in the wider culture: whether they be ramps outside pub-lic buildings, stickers affirming the dignity of the disabled, or government White Papers re-defining policies of community care. Can our sign live as it interacts and responds?

Clearly this is a very difficult question and will not be resolved in a couple of short paragraphs. What I want to register, however, is that the question is real, and the vitality of the sign we call baptism is at stake as we answer it. Perhaps my own tradition needs to do some listening to other strands in the history of the baptismal sign, to hear about ways that cognitive response can be balanced with other emphases; for example, it needs to complemented by ideas of welcome and solidarity within a community. This is, of course, a high-risk strategy for those of us bound up with this particular strand in the history of this sign, and we have good reason to be nervous. A much-loved tradition appears vulnerable to loss; but I become increasingly confident that vulnerability and growth go hand in hand. I cannot see how our version of this sign can continue to flourish unless it discovers ways by which to affirm the full and complete humanity of those with learning disabilities, a humanity that is severely brought into question if no appropriate moment for baptism can be identified within the overall span of a life journey. This will entail serious theological endeavour, for it demands the re-making of a hard-won and well-formed worldview.

My second example takes up an issue of marginalization too, one around which a cultural shift is very significant at the present time. I speak of shifting attitudes toward gender, and especially attitudes to the status of women. The point at issue here is that any sign that exclusively employs the salvation image of second birth, or rebirth, is at the same time also in danger of devaluing first birth. This is, as it were, the shadow-side of the highly affirming use of birth imagery rightly identified in chapter 3 of this book as a peculiarly significant contribution from women to the theology of baptism. In the shadow are challenges that can be directed at paedo-baptist views of baptismal regeneration as well as some born-again motifs in my own tradition.

First, there is the tendency to create a very negative attitude toward the birth process itself and woman's place in it. I am reminded of the old practice of 'churching' the woman after a birth, and all that was implied about her uncleanness and sinfulness. Historically, attitudes toward birth have been reflected in attitudes toward the women also. Second, however, there is also the tendency to devalue more generally the created goodness of the material world, an issue concerning which many women have written sensitively and prophetically in recent times.[17] As is argued in chapter 3, it is important that we hear anew emphases within the symbolism of baptism that affirm creation and the goodness of the material 'stuff' of the world. I am suggesting that we should be learning this out of a

particular encounter between the sign we call baptism and a significant
cultural shift of our time.

My third example, concerning directly the issue of pluralism, is
plainly ecclesiological, and I have deliberately kept it until last. I refer to
the relatively recent context of the local ecumenical partnerships in which
believers' baptism and the baptism of infants are practised, sometimes
literally side by side.[18] Here both Baptists and others have been severely
put to the ecumenical test; but nowhere has it been more apparent how
essential it is, in just such a context, that the baptismal sign be set free
to take on fresh symbolic power for the sake of the new community that
is coming to life. Traditionalists on both sides would call it a sell-out; but
those involved in the birth would often say that the call of God upon
them to do this new thing is greater than the call to perpetuate traditions
that belonged to other times and other places.[19]

5. In Conclusion

So how do these thoughts come together in a way that says something
significant for the exploration of the sign 'baptism' at the present time?

First, it is noteworthy that two of the examples I have cited concern
issues of marginalization, a marginalization that has been generated not
least by the historic practices carried on the meaning of the baptismal
sign. Given the present cultural encounter, Baptists and others must find
models of baptismal understanding and practice that lower the barriers
between 'us' and 'them', inside and outside. We need models that are
more creation-affirming, more human-affirming, and less dependent on
the acquisition of cognitive skills.

One way forward is to stress the 'liberating' dimension in the historic
meaning of the baptismal sign, so that baptism becomes liberating from
the oppressive dualism of the internal and the external. Another way,
again explored in other chapters of this book, is to shift the focus of
identity from the boundary to the centre and to exploit, as it were, the
centrifugal energy that radiates from the Christ who shapes the baptismal
sign. What I am looking for in this analysis, however, is a more generous
pluralist attitude to the diversity of baptismal traditions currently present
within the Christian churches. I can no longer work, for example, with
a stark and uncompromising contrast between believers' baptism, which
is right, and infant baptism, which is wrong. Rather, I am discovering

here two histories of the one sign we call baptism, both of which are proper responses to social and cultural encounters across the years. Each has about it an integrity: both in the sense of self-contained authentication, and in the sense of serious and responsible scholarship.

These histories simply cannot be mixed, nor should one be allowed to replace the other; for, in both these ways, the proper integrity of each would be destroyed. Instead, both must be valued and sensitively understood from within and without. I could not myself, with integrity, choose infant baptism for my children any more than I would expect someone baptized as an infant and responsibly exercising discipleship in another tradition to seek another baptism as a believer. But I would like to think that I can participate in and celebrate the integrity of what is other, without threat to what is profoundly my own.

Concerning my own Baptist tradition of believers' baptism, my prime responsibility is to see that it 'lives' in my own day. It is in danger of death when it no longer responds to the cultural challenges of the day. I sense that the keyword at the present is 'liberation', and especially in this context, liberation 'into community'. In this way baptism comes to represent an invitation to the external, to the outsider, to people with disabilities, to disadvantaged women; and it celebrates the material of creation itself. I sense that this will best be done by immersion into the traditions of others. To sift through the plethora of ideas and practices in the early centuries is to have our eyes opened to the very wide adaptability of the Christian vision of hope. I do not think that Baptist practice is likely to vanish, nor do I have any desire to desert it; but I want to see it live and develop in my own time, and I want to see it flourish alongside and not in opposition to those whose convictions are different from my own.

In these senses, then, I see baptism as essential to the identity of our Christian communities, the local communities that—after the fashion of Jesus—must make space in their congregations for outsiders of every kind, and the larger Christian community that must learn to live joyfully with its plural identity. Finally, however, I also want to say that what we make of our baptismal debate is not totally insignificant for the secure identity of the global community too, the community in which our baptismal mission is set. For, until we find ways amongst ourselves to defuse the divisive potential in our baptismal practices, we will remain fundamentally limited in our ability to contribute creatively to the greater peace of the world.

Notes to Chapter 5

[1]See J. D. G. Dunn, *Unity and Diversity in the New Testament* (SCM, London, 1977), p. 154.

[2]See *Baptism, Eucharist, and Ministry* (Faith and Order Paper 111, WCC, Geneva, 1982).

[3]See Max Thurian (Ed), *Churches Respond to BEM. Official Trespobses to the 'Baptism, Eucharist and Ministry' Text*, Vol. I (Faith and Order Paper 129, WCC, Geneva, 1986)

[4]A full account of how such works became, at least for a time, central to the study of the Old Testament can be found in J. W. Rogerson, *Myth in Old Testament Interpretation* (Walter de Gruyter, Berlin, 1974).

[5]The Baptist, R. E. O. White, addressing the issue of baptism in 1960, chose as the title for his book *The Biblical Doctrine of Initiation* (Lutterworth Press, London, 1960). The 1979 booklet that first made available the baptismal liturgies for the Anglican *Alternative Services Series 3* was called *Initiation Services*.

[6]R. J. Schreiter, *Constructing Local Theologies* (SCM, London, 1985).

[7]This was particularly well explored in connection with the eucharistic life of the Christian community in Jürgen Moltmann's book *The Open Church* (SCM, London, 1978).

[8]A brief, but helpful, account of the function of religious language and especially metaphor can be found in Maurice Wiles, *Faith and the Mystery of God* (SCM, London, 1982), chaps. 2–3. A much fuller treatment is given in Sallie McFague, *Metaphorical Theology* (SCM, London, 1982), p. 8. The sheer diversity of traditions is well documented in Paul Bradshaw, *The Search for the Origins of Christian Worship* (SPCK, London, 1992).

[9]Contrast Matthew 3:13-17 with Mark 1:9-11 and Luke 3:21-22.

[10]Contrast John 3:22-24 with John 4:2.

[11]Acts 2:38 onwards.

[12]As in *The Didache*; see E. C. Whitaker, *Documents of the Baptismal Liturgy* (SPCK, London, 1960), p. 1.

[13]See the *Apostolic Tradition of Hippolytus*, thought to have originated in Rome c. CE 215 in Whitaker, op. cit., pp. 2ff.

[14]Theodore, who died in CE 428, here represents the Syrian tradition; see Whitaker, op. cit., pp. 44ff.

[15]This would be clearly explicit in the work of a Protestant such as Wolfhart Pannenberg, or of a Roman Catholic like Karl Rahner.

[16]So it is relatively easy for David Pailin in *The Gentle Touch* (SPCK, London, 1992), pp. 139f. to dismiss what he considers to be a Baptist position at this point.

[17]This can be heard strongly in the work of someone such as Sallie McFague; see, for example, her *Models of God* (SCM, London, 1987).

[18]A Baptist, Alec Gilmore, was arguing clearly for this more than a quarter of a century ago; see, for example, his *Baptism and Christian Unity* (Lutterworth, London, 1966).

[19]This was well argued some years ago by another of the contributors to this book; see Christopher J. Ellis, 'Relativity, Ecumenism, and the Liberation of the Church,' *The Baptist Quarterly*, XXIX, April 1981, pp. 81-91.

6
Baptized—'in the Name of the Father and of the Son and of the Holy Spirit'

HAZEL SHERMAN

1. The occasion

Sitting together at the front of the congregation, the baptismal candidates wait for their turn to enter the water. They are of course participating in the worship, and the waiting takes place within that sequence. But this is a special time; others have come to share in this particular day, and it would be strange if they were not conscious of this. They are conscious too, perhaps, of those whom they would not wish to be present, representing the reality of fragmented or injured relationships despite the reconciliation through Christ that is now proclaimed. Few have been able to resist dipping their fingers in the water to test the temperature. Many in their mind's eye have gone through the range of potentially embarrassing incidents that could occur between their moving to the baptistery and leaving the water on the other side: 'will my gown rise up in the water?' 'Will my feet slip?' 'Will I speak in the wrong place?'

Preparation has been made for this service; minister and candidates have together looked at the words and their meanings, considered the great promises of Christian faith. And now overflowing grace is given, as divine faithfulness is made known and received in conscious faith by the believer. Life flows anew, and the church rejoices. But as in any sacramental act, the sublime and the ridiculous seem extraordinarily neighbourly. The banal and the profound meet within the same second's awareness, while the question 'so what?' snaps at our heels.

What we remember about the event is not necessarily its most significant part. Those whose recognition of an event is most closely tied to their ability to remember its details should be aware that they need to ask the question, 'But what did it *mean*, then and now?'; so those, in this case, baptized as adult believers need to ask this question just as much as those baptized as babies who have no clear memories of the occasion.

This involves looking again at familiar words that are common to baptismal liturgy in all the mainstream Christian traditions. However understandings are shaded, in whatsoever way the stress falls, highlighting in various ways the response of the believer to the Lord's command, the gift of God, cleansing from sin, regenerating, incorporating us into the body of Christ—at the climax of the rite come the words, '_____, I baptize you in the name of the Father and the Son and the Holy Spirit.' In Baptist churches and others that practise believers' baptism, the candidates thus named are then immersed in the water, to be drawn out to take their God-given place in the community of faith.

This is an emotionally charged moment, and rightly so. We hear the gospel call, the waters of death become the river of life, God holds us and carries us through. But what of this God? Why is it so vital that we are baptized 'in the name of the Father and of the Son and of the Holy Spirit'? Frequently these are remembered only as the words that are the prelude to the event, and the action overtakes the significance of the words in our memories. Solemnity and joy combine in the sonorous form of this declaration. It has weight. It is memorable. It sounds so much better than just 'God'. But, like George Eliot's Dolly Winthrop in *Silas Marner*, who pricked the letters 'IHS' on all her baking because they were good religious initials and would no doubt bring benefit to the eater, we may recognize the phrase 'in the name of the Father and of the Son and of the Holy Spirit' without realising and exploring the vital connection between this God, known in this way, and the life into which we are brought by our baptism.

2. Language and life—text and performance

For hundreds of years before the Council of Chalcedon articulated its definition of orthodoxy in A.D. 451, Christians were baptized in the name of the Father, the Son, and the Holy Spirit. Centuries later we too participate in the same rite, but our understanding of the doctrine involved does not simply rest on our *experience* of the overwhelming grace of God; we have learned a *language* by which we have come to interpret our experience. All too often we behave as if we were trying to prove something by defending the doctrine of the Trinity against all comers, or as if this doctrine somehow proves the Christian God, when of course it does no such thing. Doctrines do not come pre-packaged and ready-made, but have helped the church through the centuries to hold together three aspects of its life: where it has come from, where it is now, and where it is going.

To enable our discussion of the distinctively Christian trinitarian way of understanding God, we may borrow a category from the way we might talk about the Bible. One of the most helpful approaches to the canon of Scripture is to set our understanding of Scripture alongside an appreciation of what makes a 'classic'. One of the features of a classic is its enduring performance, and this is true of reading the text of Scripture. But should each performance simply be a repetition of the original score, using the original instruments; or is not faithfulness to that score best expressed by performance on the very best instruments available to the players in a different age, even though they may need to be played in a slightly different way and produce a subtly different sound?[1]

Similarly, the doctrine of the Trinity emerged over four centuries as the 'classic' Christian concept of God. If we cannot 'play it' with the same effect today, do we dismiss it—or do we recognize that each performance has to be truly contemporary, as a remembrance, not a mere repetition? When we recall the words 'Do this in remembrance of me' at the Lord's Supper, we are not doing this parrot-fashion, but offering ourselves to be made participants in the life of Jesus, who knew himself to be in relationship to God as a son is in relationship to his father. Once my words have been printed like this, however, we perceive all sorts of ambiguities in them: Any father? Any son? What is so special about this Jesus, for may we not (some may ask) all be potentially the same? Why Father? Why Son? Where is the space within the constraints of this male language to acknowledge the motherly love of God? What of the barrier to faith for those who cannot recognize ultimate saving significance in God incarnate manifest only in the masculine flesh of this particular Son?

If worship of God calls us only to repeat the proper words, we would be justified in blocking these questions from our minds. If the questions have not occurred to us, we may refuse to be affected by the perplexity of those women and men for whom they *have* become a problem. But vain repetition has never been a hallmark of true worship in which we offer our whole being to the grace and mercy of God. It is not enough to say, 'Talk about God as Father does not bother me. . . . I know that God is not an old man in the sky', if by doing that we are refusing to acknowledge the intimate connection between language and life and belittling the experience of those for whom the patriarchal assumptions within the church have obliterated the Christian gospel. The point of a classic is that it provokes new performances in new ages.

So we are baptized in the name of the Father, and of the Son, and of the Holy Spirit. We should beware of supposing some sort of 'original purity' in the language of trinitarian doctrine, as if a pure truth could somehow be extracted from the language itself. It is tempting to use this as a sort of device to enable us to maintain the orthodox concept of the Trinity named as Father, Son, and Holy Spirit; we might then blame abusive development of the doctrine on the generations after some 'golden age' of Christian theology when the ground rules were set down. Undoubtedly, the doctrine of the Trinity has been idolized to conform to human ways of being powerful in the world,[2] but this tendency has been there from the beginning. Unless we were to believe in the existence of a religious language that is essentially different from the words we use to communicate and develop other ideas, we must recognize that the words we use about God are the same words that we use about everything else.

But if we believe that the Christian classic of the triune God is a harmony that will echo beyond the end of time, we should not be afraid of the fact that it has not always been played, or even composed, in a way that does justice to God and to God's image in humanity, and we will look for ways of sharing in the harmony in our own generation.

3. The God who breaks all bounds

First of all, we recognize that the revelation of God to the Hebrew people is that of a God of superabundance, a God in whom there is more, always bounds-breaking, never revealed in simple undifferentiated entirety. The great 'I AM' revealed to Moses is never 'I AM in isolation'. Though jealous of His unique creating and sustaining relationship with His people and brooking no rivalry from other would-be gods, God's uncontainable being is at times expressed as a plural subject. The creative words 'Let *us* make man in *our* own image'[3] are not proof of plurality in the Godhead, but they are a sign that human beings are responding to something more than humanity can adequately respond to, and that can only be expressed in terms of relationship.[4] The thrice Holy One of Isaiah's vision[5] is the God who would also be described as working, or even playing, with His helpmate Wisdom[6], whose divine Word and Spirit express His activity in the world.[7]

There is neither space nor time here to go into the complexity of the Old Testament witness to God, but rather to remind ourselves that we find throughout the Scriptures the requirement to speak about a bounds-breaking God, and the resources to engage in this. It is significant that God who is without limits is not impersonal amorphous presence spread about without distinction. This boundless God is the same God who forges order from chaos by creative Word.

If there is a new creation in Jesus Christ, inspired by the life of the Spirit, there will also be a structure in our speaking that will draw order from the potential chaos of inarticulate experience. We see the baptism of Jesus as a threefold drama of trinitarian disclosure and impetus, as the affirmation of the Father is proclaimed in the gift of empowering by the Spirit.[8] It is clear from the letters of Paul that the practice of unity and service within the church rests on trinitarian foundation[9], and the Johannine writings (especially in the 'Farewell Discourses' of the Gospel, chapters 14–17) give an exposition of the relationship between the Father and the Son into which believers will be drawn by the activity of the Spirit. None of this, however, is a fully fledged 'doctrine of the Trinity'. This was drawn out during the first centuries of Christian history with creativity and not without controversy, as current language was stretched and shaped to respond to boundless challenge and endless hope.

The Arian controversy, rumbling on from about A.D. 318, was played out as a dispute about the status of the Son in relation to the Father, but it was also a dispute about the source and nature of salvation. The Arian camp maintained a conservative desire to defend the sole sovereignty of God, and so stressed the need for human creatures to be saved by the mediation of a creature like themselves. However, Athanasius' understanding of Christ became 'orthodox' as it affirmed that the very fullness of God, not a mere secondary level of being or divine ambassador, involved Himself in the world to accomplish redemption.

Biblical vocabulary provided fuel for this conflict rather than material for its resolution, and for the Council of Nicaea in A.D. 325 the acceptance of the non-biblical term *homoousios* ('of one substance or being') became the criterion for orthodoxy. Fifty-five years later, the Council of Constantinople confirmed that the Spirit is also 'of one substance'. The terms had been set out and a language created, but questions remained. If each person of the Trinity is *homoousios*, what is the point of distinction between them? The Cappadocian Fathers[10] helpfully spoke about the persons being distinguished in terms of their relations with one another: in God there are three *hypostases* (persons) in one *ousia* (substance), distinct in their mutual relationships.

Language is a tool that requires structure and limitation to be meaningful, however much it might point beyond its limits. The development of doctrine can be likened to a matrix[11] of language that on one boundary is restricted by a lack of courage and on the other overreaches itself in proud confidence. It has been said at times that the words we use in religion also use us, and if we speak the language of trinitarian doctrine we should be particularly alert to the ways in which we are being formed by it. The development of Trinitarian theology sets out the boundaries for our talking about God: in this way, and in these terms, we make bold to say, 'This is our God. God, who makes our baptism eventful, is like this.' This is the God of superabundance, in whom and by whom the occasion of baptism becomes an event.

4. The meaning of persons

It is sometimes suggested that trinitarian worship moves us from that which is potentially Christian in its expression to that which is fully Christian. From time to time we do need to be reminded that we can slip back into what is potentially rather than fully Christian. Focus on the Father alone restricts the Son and Spirit to 'walk-on parts' in the drama of salvation and fails to reflect the wonderful diversity in God's dealing with creation. But if, on the other hand, our relationship with Jesus takes precedence over our relationship with God we too easily find that the Jesus to whom we can relate is most like ourselves: 'What a friend we have in Jesus' becomes a private source of comfort who is too near to us to be able to challenge us. As for the Spirit, we all know of the dangers of making our God one of experience alone, by which we clothe our thought processes and psychological dispositions with divine authority. So we need a fully trinitarian 'balance' at the heart of the moment of Christian initiation to prevent us from starting off with the resources for an unbalanced view of God.

But the Trinity is not simply the formulation of a sort of insurance policy to prevent us going overboard in one direction or another. It is not a giant elastic band that pulls us back when we stray too far in one direction. As we are baptized into the fellowship of Christ in the love of God

by the power of the Spirit, we encounter God as Trinity, not as specula-
tive theology for its own sake, but as the great 'Given' that informs and
inspires the quest for unity and humbles us in the realization that God is
contained neither by us nor by our communities.

How God exists must be determinative for the existence of the
church and how that existence is formed and expressed. Therefore, it is
of vital importance for us to be aware how baptism 'in the name of the
Father and of the Son and of the Holy Spirit'—that is, in the name of a
God who is never less than personal—effects and affects our lives as
Christians, both in our communities at local level and in relationship with
one another across religious boundaries. It is distinctively Christian to encounter God as 'three persons'. It is also distinctively Christian to affirm
this emphatically whilst being quite unaware of the ambiguity inherent
in the language! It is not entirely clear to us what the Church Fathers
meant when they spoke of the three 'persons' of the Trinity, for modern
English has no exact equivalent of the Greek terms *prosopon* or *hypostasis*, or the Latin *persona*. What is absolutely clear, nevertheless, is that
each of the expressions of God communicating with us as Father, Son,
and Holy Spirit are not simply 'modes of communication' or appropriate
dress donned for particular occasions.

So we are baptized in the name of the Father, the Creator; in the
name of the Son, who receives his life from the Father and lays it down
in loving service for the world; and in the name of the Spirit, who brings
to mind all these realities as the great Enabler of all living things. The
Spirit is the third personal agent within the Trinity, sharing in the being
of God before the world's existence and manifest in all creation. Thus the
Spirit is not a poor relation tagged on after the Father and the Son, but
'the Lord, the Life Giver'. This descriptive phrase was incorporated in
the Creed of the Council of Constantinople in A.D. 381. The Spirit is recognized, not solely as enabler or mediator, but as Lord—in which we
recognize Jesus—and as Life Giver—in which we recognize the Father.
If the Spirit is the giving one, the gifts of the Spirit are those gifts of God
the Father that He has bestowed on the Son and that in turn we receive
from him.

When we talk of the importance of using personal language about
God, and when we seek to recover and interpret for our own age the
notion of *hypostasis* that has formed part of the distinctively Christian
grammar of faith since its construction early in the first centuries of the

Christian era, we should be clear what we are *not* saying. We are not using 'people' language. Misunderstandings in this area still leave much scope for caricature. We still need to make it clear that we are not envisaging the 'three persons' as if they were 'three people' in the Trinity.

We are not using 'personal' here in its currently popular sense of a 'private individual', as in a 'personal stereo'—which is something that the individual listens to on his or her own without outside interference, or as in the phrase 'it's a personal matter'— which generally translates as 'Mind your own business' or 'Keep out!' Statements may also be made 'on a personal level' or 'personally' by figures in public life, where the term 'personal' is used as a sort of shorthand to give a signal that what they are about to say may not be the official line or may differ in certain respects from the body or organization that they represent. 'Personal' here has to do with something off-the-record, indicating something of a gap between an individual and that which they represent.

When 'personal' language used of God carries shades of meaning of these kinds, it is no wonder that we have a recipe for confusion. As we sing 'God in Three Persons', we do not remember three people who keep themselves to themselves nor three individuals who are longing to say something differently 'on a personal level' to that which they communicate together. Rather, as we are baptized in the name of the Father and of the Son and of the Holy Spirit, we declare that each 'person' is fully divine, but that the total 'sum' of divinity is not greater than each of the three persons, for the fullness of the Godhead inheres in their participation each in the other.

Baptism in the name of the Trinity challenges our modern use of 'personal' as meaning 'individual' and turns us to ask again what it is to be made in the image of God, who is the source of individual distinctiveness, yet who is not individualistic. This leaves no room for any attitude of 'I'm in this for what I can get out of it', any sense of 'I am saved' without regard for what salvation might mean for the fellow members of my community and for the world beyond. In modern 'personal' language, the terms have shifted their sense from the ancient usage, but we still claim that this bounds-breaking God is most appropriately understood in personal terms. There is a whole range of uses in the word 'personal': Above all, we use it to affirm an immediacy and richness in relationship; and baptism in the name of the Father, the Son, and the Holy Spirit has to do with this.

So Jürgen Moltmann develops the theme of the social nature of God over against the arid monotheism of the monolithic, remote, and therefore largely disabled God of much Western theology, to find new points of connection between our faith and our life in society.[12] In the context of this God, society itself is challenged to reflect the divine society that has brought it to birth. This is the stuff of mission, when a trinitarian confession of faith is understood, not as doctrinal Sellotape, but the impetus for risky, hopeful living.

Lesslie Newbigin compares the church's use of the trinitarian formula to 'the talent buried in the sand for safekeeping rather than risked in the commerce of discussion'.[13] As he puts it, Christian mission is our involvement in proclaiming the Kingdom of the Father, sharing the life of the Son, and bearing the witness of the Spirit. But what does this mean, apart from playing with words?

Actually, it would do no harm at this stage to pause and reflect that 'play' is a vital activity. As adults, we generally show little perception of the value and vitality of play; we look back nostalgically to days when 'only playing' was our main activity. Yet we were not 'only playing', and neither are the children whom we see playing at relationships and using their imaginations in structuring new worlds. Play is a time of experiment and growth, and when we forget that, as children before God, our growth will be enabled by our play, we begin to stagnate.

So we might 'play' with the implications of the three persons of the Trinity in mission. The Father has freely created all things, and we stand with others within His created world. We may not invest the world with divine status, for God has invested it with created being. We aim to live responsibly within it, not to worship it. This is part of mission. We proclaim the Kingdom, which Jesus embodied, bringing liberation by his death and resurrection. Such an embodiment presents to us the heart and personal history of God. The Spirit is given, and the personal history of God is proclaimed at the heart of the world.

The artist and the theologian together may help us in our play. In the preface to his book *The Trinity and the Kingdom of God*, Moltmann reflects on the famous fifteenth-century icon of the Trinity painted by Andrei Rublev:

Through their tenderly intimate inclination towards one another, the three Persons show the profound unity joining them, in which they are

one. The chalice on the table points to the surrender of the Son on Golgotha. Just as the chalice stands at the centre of the table round which
the three Persons are sitting, so the cross of the Son stands from eternity
in the centre of the Trinity. Anyone who grasps the truth of this picture
understands that it is only in the unity with one another which springs
from the self-giving of the Son 'for many' that men and women are in
conformity with the triune God. He understands that people only arrive
at their own truth in their free and loving inclination towards one
another.[14]

This kind of God is the God who sends us *out*, as at the same time we
are drawn *into* the divine life.

5. Baptism as participation in God

To be baptized in the threefold name is to be involved in relationship and
mutual giving and receiving at the heart of the Godhead. But one of the
stumbling blocks that remains for us when we start to tease out the implications of this, is the problem of creating a whole series of pictures and
analogies that are rather too easy to make but more difficult to live by;
we may build an attractive model that in the end only leads us to despair
because it is impossible to follow. Therefore we must find new ways of
remembering that in baptism we are not simply presented with a model
to copy; we are immersed into the ongoing life of God in the world, who
has covenanted with us, not to make life easy, but to bring us to life.

There is no real imitation without participation. We are not simply in
the business of copying a model. The baptismal formula is dynamic, for
we are baptized *in the name* of the Father, the Son, and the Holy Spirit.
What's in a name? Twentieth-century Western culture may apparently
take no great account of the significance and meaning of names, yet we
still react against derogatory 'name-calling' and find it hard to respond
positively to someone who consistently forgets or mistakes our name.
There is a connection between identity and name that we can recognize
as distant relation to the passionate conviction that name and nature are
intertwined, that in fact there is everything in a name. Christian baptism
is baptism into the very life of God, named not in the stark otherness of
'God' but in threefold relationship. And this participation brings its
consequences:

(i) Challenging the nature of authority and notions of control

There is a differentiation within the Trinity, insofar as the Son and the Spirit find their source in the Father. It is not a hierarchy of dominance, but the resourcefulness of love—a source of life that never dries up or runs out. This is constantly in danger of being diverted into an abuse of trinitarian faith and fossilising into an authoritarian pyramid of control. Thus the trinitarian image has often been exploited by a patriarchal hierarchy, both deliberately and unconsciously. But the problem of the patriarchal language must not set the limits of discussion and perception; it calls us to see beyond this to the way the doctrine of the Trinity may function to undermine all notions of dominance, even within its cultural conditioning, and to see how Christian living may be resourced by the conviction that 'God is like this'.

For a believer to be baptized into the Trinity is not baptism into a 'controlling' God nor a God of rapid, easy solutions, but consciously and deliberately to be drawn into what has been called 'the trinitarian history of God in the world'[15] in which God both affects and is affected by what happens in the world. We dare to ask what the cross of Jesus means to God. For God to be present in the God-forsakenness of the cross gives us the courage to act when we cannot say for sure what the outcome will be, to concern ourselves with creating the environment and the possibilities for goodness to flourish, rather than creating a structure where they must and then falling into despair when they do not.

Baptism into the triune God points the way to the history that is within God and brings our lives and stories within that way of being. This has less to with a Platonic[16] sort of modelling our patterns of life on trinitarian forms and more to do with participating and sharing in the cost and glory of the cross. This *is* the 'trinitarian history of God in the world'.

(ii) Sharpening the question of the expression of Christian Unity

The one church, in which we are made members through our baptism, is the body of believers participating in the life of Father, Son, and Holy Spirit. 'Holy Trinity' is not added to the substance of this God; there is no 'One God' before the God who is communion.[17] So the people of God must walk together. That the church is one in Christ is a statement of faith made by those who believe in the transforming love and grace of God in Christ, operative in the world through the Holy Spirit who energizes the church. Aspects of unity may be found at different levels of dialogue and tolerance, but the church can only be said to be one when it is visibly working through the implications of redemption within its own fellowship, and working for the fruits of liberation in the world.

There is no justification in trinitarian faith for an attitude that prevents us from walking with other believers. Let any who seek to withdraw from the pilgrimage of 'churches together' be mindful of their baptism into God who exists only in relationship and in whose image we are formed. It is no accident that in Greek the words for 'glory' and 'image' are closely related[18]—we reflect the glory of God as we reflect God's image in the world. There are no parallel lines in the Trinity. 'You do your thing, and we'll do ours' is not sufficient. We *are* walking together; we cannot now choose not to.

Nor is there any room for 'tribalism' in our apprehension of the terms Father, Son, and Holy Spirit as we are brought to participate in the life of this God through our baptism. For instance, it is a nonsense to stand in the 'Spirit' camp and pour scorn on the 'Father' camp; yet this is in effect what has happened in many 'charismatic' versus 'traditionalist' clashes. In the limitless nature of God, there is room only for relationship: the limits of limitlessness touch our human situation.

(iii) Enabling real freedom

Baptism as a sign of entry into the people who keep company with the triune God opens the path to true personal freedom. John Zizioulas is among those who have exposed the dead end of existential[19] freedom, which can only be courageously grasped but never realized. In trinitarian faith we recognize that God freely chooses to be Father, Son, and Spirit for us, reaching out in overflowing relation. We may not put 'freedom' or 'person' one above the other in God. The Cappadocian theologians of the fourth century consistently envisaged the Father as 'cause' within the Trinity. Thus the distinctions between Father, Son, and Holy Spirit are not necessary or constrained, but caused by the freedom of the Father, who freely does not exist other than as the triune God. 'True being' exists not only as communion, but as free person, 'who freely affirms his being, his identity, by means of an event of communion with other persons'.[20] The act of baptism is a means of relating one's own existence as a believer to God who exists in this trinitarian way. As Zizioulas put it again:

> Baptism in the Trinity means entering into a certain way of being which is that of the Trinitarian God. Trinitarian theology has profound existential consequences.[21]

6. Baptized into pilgrimage

If there were a complete identity between God in the way we talk about God and God's own interior being, then in baptism into the name of the Father, Son, and Holy Spirit, we would be bound up with a God who is like this of necessity. We would not then be baptized into freedom and gratuitous overflowing love. But as we are baptized in the thrice-named One, into the economy of the Godhead, we are invited to share in the household purse as God works out His business of being God in the world.[22] We are baptized into the freedom of this God who chooses to reflect how He really is by the way in which He works His being out for us as being-in-relationship.

However, participation does not equal arrival. To be brought by baptism to share the life of the Father, the Son, and the Holy Spirit, does not contract us into membership of a kind of trinitarian club. The triune God also remains that which is different from us. One of the dangers of too enthusiastic an espousing of the interpenetrating (or *perichoretic*)[23] relations within the Godhead as a pattern for our life is that we may assume that we are an easy copy. And this is of little use when we realize again and again that we are party to stresses and perceptions that seem to find no meeting place with each other. Theological systems may not evade broken relationships. We do not automatically follow suit. God as Trinity is different from us in our creatureliness. We have not reached our destination, and to act as if we had is as much a temptation to the church at the end of the twentieth century as to first-century Christians in Thessalonica or Corinth.

The great and small ambiguities of our existence perplex us, and sometimes we even find it hard to distinguish the one from the other. Working out the dilemma of responsible ethical action in opposition to an elected but Nazi government, Dietrich Bonhoeffer quarried the distinction between 'ultimate' and 'penultimate'. He had determined that his place was to stand within his own country, sharing guilt and responsibility,[24] and in doing so he stepped over the line from legal to treasonable activity when he entered the conspiracy to kill Hitler. Without seeking to justify his own action against Hitler—Bonhoeffer was clear that justification lies with God alone[25]—he maintained that we live in the penultimate and have no sanction to act as if it were the ultimate.[26]

There is a 'sending' movement of the Trinity in the Gospel story that needs to be recognized in our baptismal practice. The Father sends and empowers the Son through the bestowal of the Spirit: this is at the beginning of the work of reconciliation, which is fulfilled in the cross and the resurrection yet is still to be completed in our lives. At each person's baptism we recognize that we live in the penultimate, not the ultimate; we are still beginning, joined in the name of the Father, the Son, and the Holy Spirit who leads us on. On each occasion we are faced with the limitations of a concrete situation and particular participants, but with no limits on the horizon of mindful living.

Along the way of this pilgrimage, in this essay I have not attempted a survey of trinitarian doctrine nor its systematic exposition. It would be better for the reader to benefit from some of the modern theologians who have made it their business to give an exegesis of the doctrine and its development. The purpose of the essay has been to reflect on some of the implications for those who have been baptized in the name of the Father, the Son, and the Holy Spirit and thus incorporated in the manner of being that is proper to God who is triune. In these three often-repeated names there is scope for more than a lifetime's investigation. For some, it may bring the challenge to live with the questions for a while longer: to live *as if* God is Trinity, in order to find in the practice of that the mystery of God who meets us in relationship. For others, it may be the challenge to loosen a desperately tight grip on the 'sign-on-the-dotted-line' mentality, to realize that they are treating 'Father, Son, and Holy Spirit' as a kind of rubber stamp for truth. They may be called to find a new kinship with all the Father's creation, heirs to its promise together with the Son who reaches out to redeem creation alienated from itself and from the Creator, fired by the Spirit who breathes life and freedom into every being.

Notes to Chapter 6

[1]Frances Young, in *The Art of Performance* (Darton, Longman and Todd, London, 1990) explores the relatedness of performance of a classic repertoire to performance of the texts of Scripture. Authentic performance depends not on repetition of notes but on entering into an interpretation that sounds in the ears and experience of performers and audience while being guided by the overall framework; text and performance are indivisible. In like fashion, we may suggest that the 'text' of Trinity does not stand apart from its performance in Christian living.

[2]This has been argued, notably, by Jürgen Moltmann in *Trinity and the Kingdom of God*, transl. M. Kohl (SCM Press, London, 1981), pp. 191-201.

[3]Gen 1:26

[4]The so-called 'plural of majesty' may also reflect ancient perceptions of the heavenly court, such as also finds distant echo in the Prologue of Job. Whatever its roots, it sounds out the theme that to speak of individuals alone is in fact to abstract from reality, which is found in relation.

[5]Isa 6:8.

[6]Prov 8:22-31.

[7]Ps 147:15ff; Wisd 16:12; Hag 2:5; Neh 9:30; Isa 63:10.

[8]Mark 1:1-11, cf. Matt 3:13-17; Luke 3:21-22.

[9]Rom 1:3f; Gal 4:4-6; 1 Cor 12; 2 Cor 13:14; Eph 1:3-14; Eph 4:4-6.

[10]Gregory of Nyssa (c. A.D. 330–395); Gregory of Nazianzus (A.D. 320–389); Basil of Caesarea (c. A.D. 330–379).

[11]I am using this word with its sense of a medium of formation and development. Language and doctrine are as closely connected as womb and foetus.

[12]See especially Moltmann, *The Trinity and the Kingdom of God*, op. cit.

[13]Lesslie Newbigin, *The Open Secret* (Eerdmans, Grand Rapids, 1978), p. 30.

[14]Moltmann, *Trinity and the Kingdom of God*, op. cit., p. xvi.

[15]Moltmann exploits N. Berdyaev's insight into a 'history within God': see *The Trinity and the Kingdom of God*, op. cit., p. 46.

[16]The Platonic view of the world and qualities within it considered it to be made up of a series of earthly copies of ultimate realities. The neo-Platonism that informed much of the outlook of the early Christian world continued this understanding of shadow-reality.

[17]John Zizioulas, *Being as Communion* (Darton, Longman and Todd, London, 1985), p. 17.

[18]*Doxa*, glory, is related to a verb that has to do with according someone their proper place or esteem; *eikon*, image, also speaks of reflecting a proper perspective.

[19]For the 'Christian existentialist', the proclamation of the Word is a constant call to decision, away from ourselves and towards all the implications of

confessing Jesus as Lord. Although there is no Christian proclamation without an existential aspect (we have to hear and respond in each moment), existentia*lism* as a dogma can collapse the significance of past and future within the present moment, and elevate personal response and motivation above receiving that which is done for us.

[20]Zizioulas, *Being as Communion*, op. cit., p. 18.

[21]John Zizioulas, 'The Doctrine of God the Trinity Today: Suggestions for an Ecumenical Study' in A. I. C. Heron (Ed.), *The Forgotten Trinity. A Selection of Papers Presented to the BCC Study Commission on Trinitarian Theology Today* (BCC/CCBI, London, 1991), p. 19.

[22]The analogy here stems from the term *oikonomia*, with its links with the household administration. There is an intimacy within this idea that is often missed, and this is what I intend to underline here.

[23]Perichoresis is the technical term for the concept that each person is indwelt by the other, the activity of each being therefore the activity of the one God.

[24]Bonhoeffer wrote to Reinhold Niebuhr in June 1939, 'I will have no right to participate in the reconstruction of Christian life in Germany after the war if I do not share the trials of this time with my people'. Cit. Eberhard Bethge, *Dietrich Bonhoeffer. A Biography* (Collins, London, 1977), p. 559.

[25]See Bethge, op. cit., p. 46.

[26]Dietrich Bonhoeffer, *Ethics*, transl. N.H. Smith (SCM, London, 1963), ch. IV, 'The Last Things and the Things before the Last'.

7
A Response: Anglican Reflections

CHRISTOPHER ROWLAND

It has been a welcome, if salutary, process to read this collection of essays written by representatives of Baptist churches in Britain. It has enabled me to reflect upon compromises made and contradictions lived with regarding the whole question of baptism, which I am aware have lain dormant for many years now.

1. A personal history

When I was first asked to comment on this collection, I do not know whether the contributors knew that they were asking an erstwhile crypto-Baptist who has never entirely shed these sympathies. I include this because it is important for readers to know how I am approaching this subject as there may be an expectation that I shall comment on it from the perspective of mainstream Anglican belief and practice. Of course, as a priest of the Church of England, an important part of my own preparation for priesthood in my church was coming to terms with the practice of infant baptism as the normal pattern of initiation. While it is true that there has been in recent years a lively debate about the propriety of Anglican practice, when I was preparing for ordination, I had to recognize that I would have to reach a compromise between my deeply held beliefs about the appropriateness of believers' baptism and the practice of infant baptism—which is not only the norm in the Church of England but also a defining principle of its ecclesiology.

Over the years I have come to appreciate the pattern of baptism and confirmation as an initiation rite that when sensitively used is a satisfactory way of maintaining that balance between God's grace and human response that is such a central element in the gospel. Having said that, however, I have not shed those deeply held beliefs about believers' baptism that have been a central part of my theology ever since I began to think about my faith as a teenager. My wife likewise shared these beliefs, and we made the difficult decision twenty years ago not to have our children baptized as infants. There was understandably a great deal of misunderstanding about it when our children were infants, particularly from Anglican friends and colleagues.

I look back now and on the whole have few regrets about our decision, though I think that if I were making the decision today I might be more sympathetic to the traditional pattern of initiation in my church. Of our four children, two have been baptized as young teenagers. Both occasions were powerful religious experiences. Preaching the sermon at my daughter's baptism and then performing the rite were moments never to be forgotten. The fact that it was not by immersion hardly affected the emotional and spiritual impact on her and me (not to mention others who were present) that will remain with me throughout my life. In writing this, I am aware of the danger of allowing emotion to determine theology, though equally it would be wrong to deny the extent to which such experiences have conditioned my theological outlook.

Having read through the preceding essays carefully, I have used them as a starting point for reflections that at various points engage directly with issues raised by the essays themselves. I have decided on this strategy partly to avoid the rather pedestrian sequence typical of an extended book review, and partly because I think that a constructive engagement with the issues raised by the essays demands a more open and less defended critical posture than that of the conventional respondent to academic papers. Nor do I pretend to be a kind of theological referee adjudicating the stances taken. As I have already indicated, my approach is rather one of critical solidarity with the positions adopted in these essays.

2. Placing the child in the midst

Let me continue on a personal note. The main disappointment about the essays, with which I found myself in substantial agreement, was the lack of any wisdom about how Baptists deal with the practical problems of children who are brought up in a Christian household without being baptized as infants. I still feel unease at the questioning and perplexity expressed by my children when they knew that something was denied to them that others had received and, what is more, that their father was offering to other children what he did not give to them. All this was the expected burden of an Anglican dissenter. Yet the whole area of Christian pedagogy and the place of baptism in it was a matter that I wanted to hear more about from those who have had centuries of experience of dealing with it. In an age when Christian identity has become a more significant component of the Church of England as well as other denominations (as is evident in the prolegomenon to the baptism service in the *Alternative Service Book*, 1980), the Baptist experience is one that many would like to hear about and surely benefit from.

A favourite passage in the armoury of supporters of infant baptism is the repeated welcome of children by Jesus of Nazareth (e.g. Matt 19:13; cf. 18:2f). It deserves to be examined here because it raises questions about adulthood and the wisdom of God that we submit to in baptism. I want us to think more seriously about the priority we often give to the experience of adults as determinative of an appropriate Christian response, a caution echoed by the essayists in the distinction they make between adult and believers' baptism. It is a 'childish' experience that is actually at the heart of the meaning of a Christian response, and that raises questions about any attempt to over-intellectualize the act of faith, a point that is stressed by several passages in Matthew's Gospel.

In Matthew 18, the disciples ask Jesus who is greatest in the Kingdom of Heaven. He answers by taking a child and instructing the disciples to become like the young person he has set in the midst of them. To do that is to understand what greatness in the Kingdom of Heaven means. In Matthew 18:5, Jesus is portrayed as speaking of the children as 'these little ones.' Response to the child or 'the little one' is the same as response to Jesus. Just as elsewhere in the Gospel, fulfilling the needs of the hungry and the thirsty means acting in that way to the heavenly Son of Man (25:33ff), so receiving a child means receiving Jesus (18:5).

There is something special about the child, therefore. Children, of course, are important in the Bible. They continue the race and are a sign of hope. But often in relation to their elders they are portrayed as inferior, and their responsibility is to continue in the tradition of the fathers. The exemplars of childhood are those who are obedient. The instructions to sons (and the advice is directed to sons and not to daughters) in the book of Proverbs encapsulate the subordinate role of the child. The ideal child is full of folly that is like a liquid in a container that needs to be destroyed and replaced with something more wholesome. Only when the child has undergone that cleansing and has imbibed that which is necessary for proper understanding of the world, will wisdom be achieved. All this is directed by the wise parent whose role it is to start the child 'in the way he should go,' a way of looking at children that is all too prevalent today. Being a child is to be inferior, therefore, for the child has to be inculturated into 'proper' ways of looking at the world; the child needs to be drained of immaturity and filled with adult wisdom.

What a contrast to the action of Jesus in the Gospels! The child now moves to centre stage. To place a child in the midst of the disciples is to challenge the assumption that the child has nothing of worth and can only be heeded when it has received another's wisdom. The ordering of things in the adult world is not offered as the embodiment of wisdom, for it may in fact, in some circumstances, be a perversion of it. Identification with the child and solidarity with the humble are marks of greatness. That is no easy matter, for it not only risks ridicule but also suffering and persecution. To be a child is to be at the mercy of the powerful (as is seen in Matthew's Gospel by Herod's action in slaughtering the innocents in his ruthless pursuit of the infant Jesus) and to be despised by the sophisticated (note the attempts by the ruling elite to keep the children quiet in the Temple in Matt 21:15f). Children may not have the sophistication of the learned and wise, but they do have an insight that has to be cherished and not repressed or despised.

Surprisingly, it is not the powerful, the wise, or even the disciples who recognize Jesus in Jerusalem. It is the children and the blind and lame in the temple; they are the 'little ones' who believe in him (cf. Matt 18:5). They are the ones referred to in Matthew 11:25f who are the oppressed, whom Jesus summons to himself. This group includes all those who are burdened by illness, exclusion, and oppressed by their physical or spiritual condition, who can catch a glimpse of wisdom that the sophisticated resolutely refuse to see and perversely misinterpret. They are on the margins of society, ground down by labour or victims of impoverishment or illness. They glimpse the identity of the one who is in solidarity with them. They can even stand over against the disciples as a pattern, all the more necessary when it is remembered how those adults can so easily end up on the side of Satan (Matt 16:23) and indeed find themselves betraying the Son of Man (Matt 26:14).

Those who receive these insights into the divine wisdom are marginal and humble, both in terms of status and circumstances. They are privileged, however. In glimpsing the significance of Jesus they have seen something hidden from the wise and the sophisticated. Their perspective does represent a challenge to those who think that they know how to understand scripture and the world, when in fact the secret is hidden from them. Identification with them, and with the child in particular as the representative of those who are in worldly terms humble, is an imperative for the disciple.

All this raises searching questions for me about the nature of our provision for children in liturgy and common life and the extent to which those of us who are adults recognize children as persons of importance within the Christian fellowship. There are various issues here. First, as I shall go on to suggest, if the church is in some sense an alternative to prevailing culture and ideology, how do we provide alternatives for children who find themselves as the result of peer pressure compelled to conform (as do we all of course)?

Second, there is the necessity for adults with the care of children to provide an environment that will enable them to learn ways of relating that break the inherited cycle of behaviour that demeans and disfigures children, simply because the child in every adult has herself been the victim of various forms of demeaning and oppressive behaviour. Merely providing catachesis for children, without adults themselves being open to and offering each other ways of breaking the destructive power that belittles the child, is to ignore the major part of the problem posed by inherited patterns of behaviour from which salvation in Christ offers liberation.

3. A liturgical perspective

When we are offered a Baptist perspective on the issue of Christian initiation, an omission in the essays is the lack of an engagement with the common theological tradition of Baptists as represented in their forms of worship, for example in the form of baptism recommended by the Baptist Union, which is surely one element of the identifying characteristics of Baptist faith and practice. In exploring this I recognize that many Baptists would regard such texts as guidance rather than prescriptive formularies. However, let me illustrate the importance of this by reference to the baptism services of my church, the Church of England.

No greater doctrinal change is apparent in the liturgy than in the service of baptism. A comparison between the liturgy of the *Book of Common Prayer* (BCP) and the *Alternative Service Book* (ASB) reveals that there has been an abandonment of a doctrine of original sin that requires baptism as the necessary antidote to imminent perdition. The modern service stresses the duties of parents and godparents to bring up the child in the Christian faith, whereas the *BCP* starts by asserting that 'all men are conceived and born in sin', so that a person needs baptism in order to receive 'that thing which by nature he cannot have'. The point is made even more clearly in the catechism where the one to be confirmed affirms that 'he is a child of wrath.' In the order of baptism 'for those of riper years', the preface affirms that 'all men are conceived and born in sin (and that which is born of the flesh is flesh), and they that are in the flesh cannot please God but live in sin, committing many actual transgressions.'

The assumption is also made in this service that the person who is baptized will in due time come to confirmation. Baptism of children is explained in the atechism in the following way: 'Why then are infants baptized, when by reason of their tender age they cannot perform them [i.e., repentance and faith]?' Answer: 'Because they promise them both by their sureties; which promise, when they come to age, themselves *are bound to perform*' (my italics). That assumption is more easily understood in an era when the one baptized would be part of a Christian culture and when there would be the expectation that in general terms the society would be informed by Christian values. That is no longer the case. The baptism of an infant may not be conditional on the one baptized ratifying at confirmation the vows made on his or her behalf, but its effects *are* dependent on appropriate pedagogy for the proper outcome of the baptismal initiation. The initial exhortation to parents and godparents in the *ASB* suggests an implicit acceptance that the path to confirmation is one that is dependent on the provision of that environment, which will ensure the delivery of a Christian culture as an essential context for the fulfilment of that goal.

Now I recognize that it is dangerous to project the experience of uniformity, which historically has been so typical of Anglicanism and Roman Catholicism, on to the more congregational ecclesial arrangement of Baptist churches. Nevertheless, a glance at collections published by the Baptist Union of Great Britain to give liturgical guidance may be expected to reflect the ethos of baptismal practice and theology. There is much that is common, particularly the declaration of faith and baptism in the name of the Trinity, but two differences are worth noting. First, the pre-baptismal prayer in the Baptist *Patterns and Prayers for Christian Worship* may be contrasted with the similar prayer in the Anglican liturgy:

Patterns & Prayers

Almighty God, we give you thanks that at the beginning your Spirit moved upon the face of the waters and you said, 'Let there be light.' We give you thanks that you led your people through the water of the Red Sea, out of slavery, and into the freedom of the Promised Land.

We give you thanks for your Son, Jesus Christ, who was baptized in the river Jordan. We thank you that he passed through the deep waters of his death on the cross and was raised to life in triumph. Send your Holy Spirit that this baptism may be for your *servants* a union with Christ in his death and resurrection that, as Christ was raised from death through the glory of the Father, *they* also might live new lives. Send your Holy Spirit anew upon *them* that *they* may be brought into the fellowship of the Body of Christ and may grow in Christ's likeness.[1]

Alternative Service Book

Almighty God, whose Son Jesus Christ was baptized in the river Jordan, we thank you for the gift of water to cleanse us and revive us; we thank you that through the waters of the Red Sea, you led your people out of slavery to freedom in the promised land; we thank you that through the deep waters of death you brought your Son, and raised him to life in triumph.

Bless this water, that your *servants* who *are* washed in it may be made one with Christ in his death and resurrection, to be cleansed and delivered from all sin. Send your Holy Spirit upon *them* to bring *them* to new birth in the family of your Church, and raise *them* with Christ to full and eternal life. For all might, majesty, authority, and power are yours, now and for ever.[2]

In an alternative prayer provided in the Baptist order, baptism is seen
as a moment when 'they signify their desire to follow your Son' and as
an 'important step on their lives' journeys' that may 'wash away the fears
and sins of the past.' Compared with the Anglican liturgy, the Baptist liturgy remains more vague about the character of the sacramental act. In
the Anglican prayer there is an invocation for God's blessing on the stuff
of water that will act as the means of the transfer from death to life, and
provide the moment of identity with those moments of deliverance in
salvation history alluded to in both prayers. An outsider may be forgiven
for supposing that the phrase in *Patterns and Prayers* 'Send your Holy
Spirit that this baptism may be for your servants a union with Christ'
suggests a form of words that can encompass those who might differ
among themselves on the nature of baptism as a sacrament and as an
effectual means whereby newness of life in the Spirit may be engendered.

A similar difference concerns the act of signing with the cross and
the brief allusion to 'exorcism' in the words that follow in the Anglican
liturgy: 'May almighty God deliver you from the powers of darkness, and
lead you in the light and obedience of Christ.' Even in the Anglican liturgy this is a truncated form of a much longer prayer still present in
modern Roman Catholic baptismal liturgy in the prayer:

> Almighty and ever-living God, you sent your only Son into the world
> to cast out the power of Satan, spirit of evil, to rescue man from the
> kingdom of darkness, and bring him into the splendour of your kingdom
> of light. We pray for this child: set him (her) free from original sin,
> make him (her) a temple of your glory, and send your Holy Spirit to
> dwell with him (her).[3]

There then follows the anointing that is a reminder of the early
church's catechumenate. This part of the baptism rite takes place some-
where different from the baptistery, indicating the movement from one
culture to another (an issue to which we shall have to return later in the
essay).

The origin of this goes back to our earliest baptismal liturgy. So for
example in the *Apostolic Tradition* of Hippolytus, which may reflect liturgical practice in the Roman church at the end of the second century
A.D., there is a clear notion of the baptism as the moment of transference
from the realm of 'the prince of this world' to a new dispensation under
God. My reason for pointing this out is that the theological concern of

this disturbing language, at first sight, is very much at one with the concerns of the Baptist authors of the present essays; they want to stress the importance of the material means of the experience of God's grace and the notion of a change of life that involves a deliverance or liberation from a pattern of life contrary to the way of God. This deliverance is more than individual; it is institutional and cultural. Is there then a case for recognizing the importance of the deliverance that baptism both speaks of and effects in any revision of recommended liturgies in the future?

4. A positive attitude to our sectarian roots?

Sectarianism has a negative flavour in Christian circles. On occasion in these essays there is an apologetic note sounded whenever there is any suggestion that Baptist practice recommends sectarianism. Baptists should not be apologetic about getting us establishment Christians to face up to our own sectarian inheritance and should not concede the moral high ground to those who claim to be inclusive and less discriminating in their baptismal practice.

I am not necessarily ignoring the many advantages in terms of Christian evangelism that the inclusive approach of the Anglican church has offered through the ages. Rites of passage are important, and that service offered by a national church is not without its theological propriety. Nevertheless, the sectarianism that we all so much balk at is endemic in the baptism service—perhaps more so here than in other acts of worship in the church, the Eucharist included. At the heart of the service is a dualistic pattern of thought that accurately encapsulates the notion of transfer from one kind of allegiance to another. Boundaries are set more clearly here than at almost any other moment in Christian worship. The person baptized moves from darkness to light, from the realm of the powers of evil to the realm of God. There is a passage through water, a cleansing and a newness, all effecting a boundary that has to be crossed. In the actions and words of the baptismal liturgy the cost of discipleship is most clearly enunciated.

Such patterns of thought and action are characteristic of groups with clear boundaries. In the sociology of religion, the *sect* has been contrasted with the *church*. The latter is the all-embracing body whose boundaries are blurred, and which makes it possible for those on the fringes to exist comfortably on the margins with only fragile or nominal commitment. The sect is different, however. It has rules of membership. The boundary between insiders and outsiders is relatively clear. In the baptism service there is kept alive the sectarian character of Christianity. It started life as a form of sectarian Judaism, which clearly defined boundaries on the basis of belief and practice. Emerging Christianity until the time of Constantine was characterized by such a sectarian spirit. This is well brought out in Wayne Meeks' book *The Origins of Christian Morality*.[4] The catechumenate was long and thorough, putting to shame our lack of rigour in baptismal preparation. But at the heart of the whole baptismal experience was the clear message of transfer from one dominion to another involving the acceptance of Jesus Christ as king of kings and lord of lords.

Even after the church became the religion of the state, the rites of initiation have kept alive the sectarian spirit, which is of the essence of Christianity, doing justice to which is a central feature of our theological task. For this reason I have often wondered whether the church is right to make the Eucharist the 'exclusive' rite while being more all-embracing in its baptismal practice. I can see a case can be made (notwithstanding the tradition of the church) for Christian communities to offer an open table to which all who wish may be invited to share in the eucharistic fellowship, while reserving the service of baptism for those who wish to be committed to that pattern of life that they glimpse in the fellowship of the eucharist.

5. Challenging exclusivism

If I have thus far stressed the importance of attending to our sectarian inheritance, which I think the Baptist tradition seeks to uphold, I want to explore the proper reservations, which people have expressed about the exclusivism, particularity, and tendency to moral superiority that sectarianism can engender.

Commentators on the New Testament have often said that there is so little apparent concern with the wider world. The sectarian spirit seems to manifest itself in a fatalistic acceptance of the status quo and an unwillingness to get involved in politics and change society. But what is so striking about the New Testament texts is that they were written by people who had little or no political power, with a vision of the world, which was at odds with the prevailing ideology. Yet their countercultural stand did not mean that they ended up writing utopian tracts that were far removed from their everyday reality. We may not like their lack of explicit condemnation of slavery or the subordination of women, but there are enough indications that the status quo could not simply be maintained to suggest that they propounded and expected a different kind of understanding of, and way of living in, the world.

There was always a temptation for self-righteousness, to see the world 'out there' as in some sense corrupt and contrasting with the pool of life that was the Christian *ecclesia*. The New Testament is full of that kind of dualistic language, and we may be pardoned for supposing at first that the early Christians thought of God's presence being only with the community of believers. But it is not only the Pentecost account of Acts, which talks of the Spirit being poured on all flesh, that challenges this since the most 'sectarian' document in the New Testament, the Fourth Gospel, indicates that the Christian community cannot maintain a superior position with regard to the activity of the Spirit of God; the Spirit is not the church's possession, for the church too is under the judgement of God and in need of the divine mercy. That is not to deny that disciples have their role. In the Johannine Farewell Discourses, the disciples are said to be the witnesses to the departed Christ. But that witness will be alongside the activity of the Spirit-Paraclete in challenging an unbelieving world (John 15:26). The process of witness is itself conditional: 'If you love me, you will keep my commandments; and I will pray the father and God will send another Paraclete, the Spirit of truth (14:13).' While the Spirit comes to the disciples and will be in them and among them because the world hates Christ and is not able to receive the Spirit, that does not deny the fact of the Spirit's activity in the world.

This is most evident in John chapter 16. The coming of the Spirit involves convicting the world of sin, of justice and judgment. In that process the Christian community may have its part, but it would be wrong to suppose that this activity will be confined to that community. The sovereign spirit is at work, if necessary entirely independent of the community of believers. They do not have a monopoly of righteousness, even though their inheritance of the story of God means that they may be best equipped to understand and to enable others to fathom the mystery of God and the world.

6. The sacrament of baptism

All this raises questions about the relationship between baptism and conversion. I think that the essayists indicate quite clearly that they are unhappy about the devaluation of the baptismal rite and want to stress its sacramental significance. The material character of the rite is a necessary corrective to the easy separation of the material and the spiritual that is such a feature of our modern world and our most distinctive contribution to the history of heresy. The experience of God through 'stuff' is of the essence of our understanding of God, and the separation of God from the ordinariness of our world is to be resisted.

Like the essayists, I too would want to stress the action of the Spirit before the moment of baptism, but equally the importance of the material as the medium of divine activity is something that should never be downplayed. In our baptismal liturgy we are affirming that baptism is not merely a sign of something that has already happened, but is itself an important moment—albeit part of an ongoing account we would want to give—of God's activity with regard to that individual and the world as a whole. Like the events to which it alludes, the death and resurrection of Jesus—which in some sense changed the world—baptism itself is more than an affirmation. It is itself an identification with those moments that changed the universe and with which an individual is herself linked in word, deed, and fellowship and thereby changed. The components of what we say *and* do bring the individual within the orbit of God's love manifested in a story told, a rite repeated, and a community committed to a way of looking at the world that reflects that story and shares the same experience. This is not to say that the community is perfect or has its understanding of the story right. Rather, when it meets together, it is committing itself afresh by putting itself under the judgment and grace of God.

So at the moment of baptism there is more than merely an affirmation of something that is already true; there is a meeting with the living God. It is an awesome and critical *kairos* that is evident in the ways in which we set our bit of history within the context of epochal events of the past: the Exodus; the life, death, and resurrection of Jesus; and the coming of the reign of God. The God who comes in judgment at the end of time meets us, not because we engineer it, but because in humility we come before the throne of justice and mercy; and as a community seeking

God's will, we offer our words and actions as a space for the understanding and conversion by God's action and grace. The action of baptism is in a real sense being brought into the ambience of God.

This is not to say that God is absent from the world 'outside'. I have already given reasons why it is important that we challenge the sectarianism that sees God at work only or even primarily in the community of the faithful. It is like the moment when one transfers from one jurisdiction to another. When I pass through customs and immigration on arriving in another country, I become subject to a different set of laws and customs. At the moment when my passport is stamped, something happens to me; my circumstances change in a way that is not immediately apparent. Baptism is similar, though much more than that happens. The grace of God has been at work long before the moment I come to the rite of passage. But in crossing the boundary into the Christian community and into an area where God's story is told and reflected upon, I come into contact with the Spirit in an explicit way. This can enable me to understand, interpret, and appropriate the promptings of the divine spirit in myself, others, and the world in a way that helps me make sense. I shall go on finding God elsewhere, perhaps even more powerfully than inside the Christian community, but at the moment of baptism God enables me to begin that process of understanding and nurture without which the Spirit is quenched.

7. Being born again

In most baptismal liturgies allusion is made to the enigmatic dialogue between Jesus and Nicodemus in the Gospel of John (3:1-12). Nowhere in the New Testament does the nature of Christian baptism receive such a profound treatment as in this narrative, replete as it is with some of the best-known verses in the New Testament, but shot through also with ambiguity that defies the interpretative skill of the most expert commentator.

The identity of the participants is significant and often missed. The strange emissary from God whose mission Nicodemus recognizes is approached by one who is a leader of the Jews. In other words, one of the persons in the group, who later in the Gospel was to be in the forefront of Jesus' denunciation to the imperial authorities, here breaks cover, and under the cover of darkness seeks out Jesus. Nicodemus, about whom we hear only in John's narrative, appears later in the Gospel as a tentative supporter of Jesus (cf. 7:50; 19:39), but one who hovers on the brink of discipleship. He comes with words of flattery. It is an approach that the Johannine Jesus ignores, confronting the leader of the Jews with the uncompromising statement that he needs to be born over again or from above (there is a play on words here, similar to 19:11). For Nicodemus to seek the Kingdom of God, he needs a complete transformation, which can only be likened to a birth. The teacher misses the metaphor and perversely persists in taking things literally. As a result of his dwelling on earthly things (3:12), he proves to be incapable of understanding the mysteries of God.

The climactic transformation that Jesus speaks of here is directed to one who is part of 'the opposition.' That opposition is not seen merely in religious terms, however, but in social and political terms also. Nicodemus is a leader of the Jews. Jesus bids him move from that position to one in which he can share the transformation of perspective, which is essential in order to be able to 'see the Kingdom of God.' His social, political, and religious positions make it impossible for him. There is the occasional hint that more than the individual religious leader is being addressed in this chapter. So in verse 7 there is the sudden change from singular to plural (just as there is in v. 12) suggesting that there is a wider social challenge mounted here in which two communities confront one another with rival views of the world.

As far as the writer of the Fourth Gospel is concerned, the true perspective is not that of the political leadership or even their Roman allies, but the minority group that followed the stranger from heaven. No wonder that we find Nicodemus never taking the plunge of baptism. That would have been a public, very political, act that would have required him to change sides. He would have had to leave behind the power of the national leadership and identify himself with one whose baptism meant initiation into a very different perspective on the world. While he remains part of the leadership and however hard he tries to distance himself from it, he is looking at the world from a purely human point of view. That is the perspective of the flesh rather than the spirit. Just as the Jesus of the synoptic Gospels had talked of solidarity with the child as the necessary condition for understanding the Kingdom and being truly great, so Nicodemus has to see that however old one may be, there is necessity to go through the process of gestation and growth that will enable a new perception. Despite being a teacher of Israel, Nicodemus cannot understand. Like many others, he thinks, hears, and understands the voice of God; but the claim is spurious (cf. 5:35). The things of earth dominate Nicodemus' outlook.

Just as Paul had talked about the contrast between human and divine wisdom, so here too the Johannine Jesus probes the way in which the lack of an appropriate epistemology means a lack of faith. That 'epistemological break' can only come about through baptism, which is itself an event that is dangerous politically and socially. So the blind man, whose conviction that Jesus is a teacher of Israel ultimately leads to ostracism and a meeting with Jesus, is excluded from society and family. Commentators have rightly pointed out the baptismal imagery in his washing in the pool of Siloam in 9:7, so that 'seeing again' means a social shift and not just a doctrinal/religious shift. The blind man's perspective is one that enables him to recognize the Son of Man, but that means a public separation from the prevailing culture. It shares the perspective of the heavenly Son of Man who himself suffered the opprobrium of the political establishment (note that it is the leaders of the Jews in John's Gospel who accuse Jesus; the crowd has no role). The position of the follower will be no different from that of the Master (cf. 15:24ff). When persons come to baptism, they enter the realm where understanding begins to be possible and their perspective on reality changes. They then see that their deeds were evil and that in the past they loved darkness rather than light.

The 'epistemological break' that involves the change of lifestyle as well as thought is brought out in a passage from Cyprian, bishop of Carthage, in which he describes the problems posed for him by conversion to Christianity and the change of practice as well as heart that resulted from baptism. As Alan Kreider[5]—who drew my attention to this—pointed out, the struggle for Cyprian in becoming a Christian was the requirement that he simplify his style of life, and it was only the powers unleashed by baptism that enabled him to do this:

> While I was still lying in darkness and gloomy night . . . and remote from truth and life, I used to regard it as a difficult matter, and especially as difficult in respect of my character at that time, that a man should be capable of being born again . . . and that a man quickened to a new life in the laver of saving water should be able to put off what he had previously been . . . 'How,' said I, 'is such a conversion possible, that there should be a sudden and rapid divestment of all which,

either innate in us has hardened in the corruption of our material nature, or acquired by us has become inveterate by long accustomed use? These things have become deeply and radically ingrained within us. When does he learn thrift who has been used to liberal banquets and sumptuous feasts? And he who has been glittering in gold and purple, and has been celebrated for his costly attire, when does he reduce himself to ordinary and simple clothing?' . . . But after that, by the help of the water of new birth, the stain of former years had been washed away, and a light from above, serene and pure had been infused into my reconciled heart,—after that, by the agency of the Spirit breathed from heaven, a second birth restored me to a new man;—then in a wondrous manner, doubtful things at once began to assure themselves to me . . . What before had seemed difficult began to suggest a means of accomplishment, what had been thought impossible, to be capable of being achieved.[6]

8. *The quest for Christian identity*

I have alluded to the Protestant suspicion of sacramental theology that is dealt with so thoroughly in the essays. But there is another area that deserves attention, for it too represents one of the challenges that confront Protestant churches as they wrestle with their Catholic inheritance. Brief allusion is made in these essays to the 'Lima Document' on *Baptism, Eucharist, and Ministry*—surely a significant indicator of where the Baptist churches stand with regard to contemporary ecumenical debate. The comment made on the document, however, indicates one of the problems that Protestant churches have to confront. Richard Kidd refers to this document and asserts:

> We Baptists, because of our ecclesiological tendency to emphasize the autonomy of local congregations, had no real mechanism for making a response anyway; inasmuch as we tried, our offering was little more than a statistical self-analysis revealing the measure of division already amongst us.[7]

Kidd despairs of the process that he fears results less in unity than in the fragmentation, which he says, 'stands in such striking contrast to the authentic spirit of the gospel.' Two points call for comment here.

First, there is a serious question here about the nature of Baptist identity when the autonomy of local congregations is so strong. What identifies a Baptist church? In what way is it possible for the Baptist Union of Great Britain to make a response to the Lima document? I speak here with no sense of superiority because the Roman Catholic Church is equally critical of the Anglican Communion's inability to respond in any coherent uniform way. The Baptist situation actually reflects the reality on the ground. That is the dilemma we face in trying to look for a common mind in the face of such a variety of vested interests. But that is part and parcel of the authenticity of the gospel whose articulation has always been the subject of conflict. I suspect that from the very start of Christianity there has been dispute about baptism. For instance, should it be in the name of Jesus alone or via the invocation of the Trinity? Should it be repeated as the lustrations commonly practised in Judaism? How did it differ from the baptism of John? There is thus to my mind no golden age of unified practice to which we can hark back even if the present state of affairs can be said to mark a significant departure from the pre-Constantinian church. Our quest for understanding is at the heart of our common task as the people of God as we look for ways of coming to a common mind. To search together despite all the strains, is to be true to and to proclaim the gospel. That seems to me to be entirely authentic and to free us from the utopian nostalgia of searching for some lost paradise of ecclesiastical bliss.

In that situation we can expect the wisdom of the social sciences to enable us to have some understanding of how we behave and how our contrasting social and political situations condition us to act in particular ways. But that resort to social analysis cannot offer us a kind of meta-narrative, 'an explanatory framework' (to use Richard Kidd's phrase). Yes, we need to attend to the differing contexts in which baptism is performed and the differing ways in which the symbols are understood. That is at the heart of a contextual theology that is faithful to the spirit of the Incarnation, but it cannot explain the totality of existence, as if there were some meta-language that enabled us to subject religion to analysis and offer explanations of the peculiar things we Christians do and say. That is not to deny the importance of listening to voices from outside looking in and observing. It is possible that we may catch the voice of the Spirit who blows where she will in all of this, though we shall not cede to our observers the right to determine that what we hold to be of the truth is merely the result of human deception.

These essays raise many issues that remind us of the neglected but central role that baptism should play in the ecumenical quest for Christian identity. Reflection on this rite, which was always, as far as we can ascertain, open to women as well as to men, can surely enable today's fragmented church to develop its understanding and experience of what we share in Jesus Christ. So it is that my Baptist friends have offered us a timely reminder of the riches of thought and life that the sacrament unfolds for the people of God.

Note to Chaper 7

[1]*Patterns and Prayers for Christian Worship. A Guidebook for Worship Leaders.* Baptist Union of Great Britain (Oxford University Press, Oxford, 1991), pp. 99-100.

[2]*The Alternative Service Book 1980. Services Authorized for Use in the Church of England.* (Oxford University Press/ A.R. Mowbray & Co Ltd, Oxford, 1980), p. 231.

[3]'The Rite of Baptism for Children', International Commission on English in the Liturgy (1969).

[4]Wayne A. Meeks, *The Origins of Christian Morality: the First Two Centuries* (Yale University Press, New Haven, 1993)

[5]Alan Kreider, 'Worship and Evangelism in Pre-Christendom,' *Vox Evangelica* 24 (1994), pp. 13-14.

[6]'Cyprian, Epistle 1 to Donatus 3-4'. Cited from *The Writings of Cyprian,* transl. R. E. Wallis, Ante-Nicene Christian Library (T. & T. Clark, Edinburgh, 1868), pp. 2-4.

[7]See above, p. 86.

In Conclusion: Continuing the Dialogue

RICHARD KIDD

With Christopher Rowland's agreement, we venture to continue the dialogue one stage further—even if only briefly. As authors we are profoundly grateful for Professor Rowland's response to our chapters, not only for his own distinctive theological contribution, but also because the resulting dialogue exemplifies a way of doing theology that we are enthusiastic to commend to others. We offered our initial thoughts with a mixture of confidence and hesitancy: confidence because they are already the fruit of sustained theological endeavour, but hesitancy because we are deeply aware of the provisionality of all theological pronouncements, and most certainly our own. As we have listened to the way our Anglican colleague 'heard' what we have written, we are challenged to think further, and sometimes to think again; and for that we are grateful. It makes us want to write some more, as we are doing here, and that can only be good. Ideally, Christopher Rowland would speak again, and so on. But the hoped-for scenario is that conversations will continue in a great variety of places beyond the pages of this book.

Turning to the detailed text of Professor Rowland's response, we were struck both by what he heard and by what he did not seem to hear at all. Most of his opening remarks concern the status and validity of infant baptism. We had thought this to be the very ground we were attempting to leave behind. Our Baptist parents in the faith had written at length against the practice of infant baptism. This rightly sharpened their own understanding of believers' baptism; we have learned a great deal from their wisdom, and firmly stand in the tradition that they shaped. We thought, however, that we had moved the discussion onto fresh ground, suggesting new areas in which the baptismal debate might release creative energy, free from its earlier impasse.

That is why our chapters focus on such themes as creation, politics, community, and above all on the nature of the triune God. Where we do speak of the contrast between infant and believers' baptism, it is within a framework of constructive affirmation, looking for ways to show deep respect for each other's traditions. We are learning, however, that it is not as easy to move onto the new territory as we thought, and it may well be that we shall need to return again to some of the older ground before we can fully achieve all we have in mind.

In particular, it is clear that we are not going to be able to talk long in an ecumenical forum about baptism and about church without working again at our theology of children. We are glad to report, as mentioned in the introduction to this volume, that this is a significant theme in the latest paper from the Doctrine and Worship Committee of the Baptist Union of Great Britain, entitled *Believing and Being Baptised* (1996). In this document a variety of models of understanding are explored, and fresh attention is given to the meaning of the act of presentation and blessing of children as practised among Baptists.

We also found it instructive to hear afresh how we, as Baptists, are seen by others, and especially by someone like Christopher Rowland who has such evident sympathies with our distinctive stance. We find it odd to see passages from the Baptist book *Patterns and Prayers for Christian Worship* set alongside others from the Anglican *Alternative Service Book*, for we know how few Baptists feel any obligation at all to work from such a text. We know only too well how the production of such books is perceived, as expressing the ideas of particular individuals and movements within a specific generation, and as drawing too freely on loved and trusted texts from other traditions. As Baptists, we would not think of doing theology from a prayer book, not even our own! We can learn something, however, from the way in which others perceive us. Perhaps we are not as honest with ourselves as we would sometimes like to think? Perhaps we ought to give closer attention to our own liturgical practices? Maybe what Baptists actually do and say at a baptism represents more about what we believe than we sometimes acknowledge.

Again we found it odd to see how we are urged to affirm our identity as 'sect'—not a way we typically choose to describe ourselves. The reasoning behind our 'apologetic note' is that we tend to hear the word 'sect' as an accusation, largely meaning 'cut off from others'—something we have no desire to be. Although technically the simple fact of our separation from the state church—something we own gladly—signals to some our identity as a sect, we prefer not to think of ourselves as 'sectarian' in any of the narrowing senses that, it feels to us, have become loaded into that term.

We are responsive to the way in which Christopher Rowland is able to use the idea of 'sectarianism' so positively, emphasizing the magnitude of the transformation implicit in the baptismal promise of allegiance to Jesus Christ. We are also challenged by the way in which he locates such sectarianism in the earliest roots of Christian believing. We suspect, however, that at the present time it is easier to own this way of speaking from within the established church than it is from outside it, given the prevailing currents of meaning.

The meaning of the word 'sectarian' remains so very slippery. If anything, in the Free Churches we would tend to think of adherents to a *state* church as those who are most in danger of being constrained by a 'sectarian' spirit; that is, in stark contrast to Christopher Rowland's use of the word, trapped within the boundaries of their own alliances and traditions. This is often how we interpret our experience at those public meetings and state occasions in British life, when we as Free Church can easily feel ourselves to be outsiders to the approved patterns of conduct and distributions of power.

Perhaps the truth of the matter is that we need another word altogether: we need one that will express both the radical dimension of loyalty and transformation we so readily applaud in Christopher Rowland's critique, and also our own determination to ride loose to the narrow boundaries of the -isms with which we are too easily encircled. What is undoubtedly fascinating and constructive is to hear how we are actually perceived by others and to learn how better to express ourselves in future.

We were surprised, but also heartened, that Christopher Rowland challenges so little of what we feel to be the substance of our chapters. In fact he builds on them for us in very helpful and creative ways, which suggest further steps that might be taken to develop their core ideas. His own wrestling with the interpretation of sacrament affirms with us the central importance of the 'stuff' of the earth, challenging us to take still more seriously what we actually say and do in the baptismal drama. His attention to the politics of faith, focused through the characters of Nicodemus and Jesus himself in the Fourth Gospel, pushes further our own testimony to the political dimension of this daring public ritual. These, and more, help to take what we saw ourselves to be doing a further stage forward.

So now it is over to others. We do not expect everyone to agree with what we have written—far from it. We ourselves will be glad to continue the dialogue, and we will be heartened to 'listen in' as others make dialogue together.

Index

W

Walton, R. C. 44n
Wesley, John 13
Wiles, Maurice 98n
Wink, Walter 82n, 83n
witness 4, 18, 19, 24, 37, 76-78
Word 37-38, 40
world 5, 42, 79, 82, 128, 129
    (*see also* Creation)
World Council of Churches 60,
    86, 132
worship 32, 41-42, 101-102,
    106, 121-23, 136

Y

Yoder, John Howard 71, 82n
Young, Frances 115n

Z

Zizioulas, John 112, 113, 116n